Buddhism

A VERY SHORT INTRODUCTION

Damien Keown is Senior Lecturer in
Indian Religion at Goldsmiths College,
University of London, and a Fellow of
the Royal Asiatic Society.

Very Short Introductions offer stimulating, accessible introductions to a wide variety of subjects, demonstrating the finest contemporary thinking about their central problems and issues.

Also available from Oxford Paperbacks

Archaeology: A Very Short Introduction
Paul Bahn

Classics: A Very Short Introduction
Mary Beard and John Henderson

Judaism: A Very Short Introduction
Norman Solomon

Politics: A Very Short Introduction
Kenneth Minogue

Forthcoming from Oxford Paperbacks

Islam: A Very Short Introduction
Malise Ruthven

Law: A Very Short Introduction
Jeffrey Jowell and Stephen Guest

Literary Theory: A Very Short Introduction
Jonathan Culler

Psychology: A Very Short Introduction
Gillian Butler

Theology: A Very Short Introduction
David Ford

A VERY SHORT INTRODUCTION

Buddhism

Damien Keown

Oxford   New York

OXFORD UNIVERSITY PRESS

1996

Oxford University Press, Great Clarendon Street, Oxford OX2 6DP

Oxford New York
Athens Auckland Bangkok Bogota Bombay
Buenos Aires Calcutta Cape Town Dar es Salaam
Delhi Florence Hong Kong Istanbul Karachi
Kuala Lumpur Madras Madrid Melbourne
Mexico City Nairobi Paris Singapore
Taipei Tokyo Toronto
and associated companies in
Berlin Ibadan

Oxford is a trade mark of Oxford University Press

British Library Cataloguing in Publication Data
Data available

Library of Congress Cataloging in Publication Data
Data available
ISBN 0–19–285329–5

10 9 8 7 6 5 4 3 2 1

Typeset by Hope Services (Abingdon) Ltd.
Printed in Great Britain
by Mackays plc,
Chatham, Kent

Contents

List of Illustrations

List of Maps

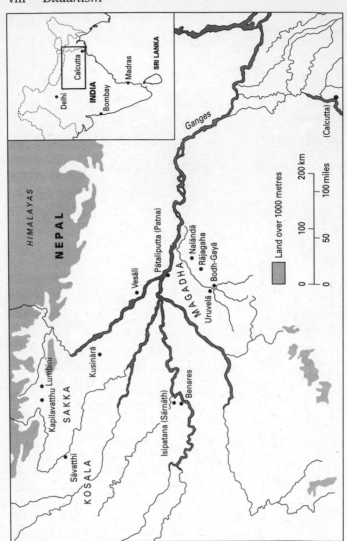

1. India and the region where the Buddha taught and lived

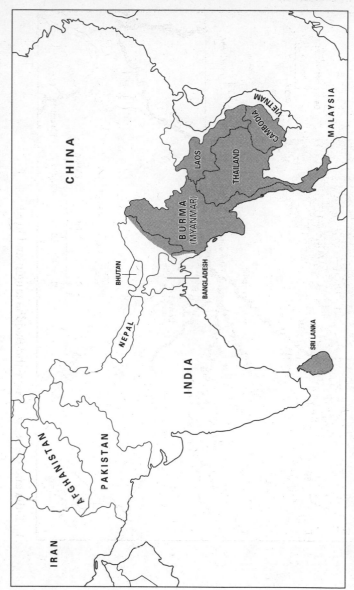

2. Theravāda Buddhism in Asia

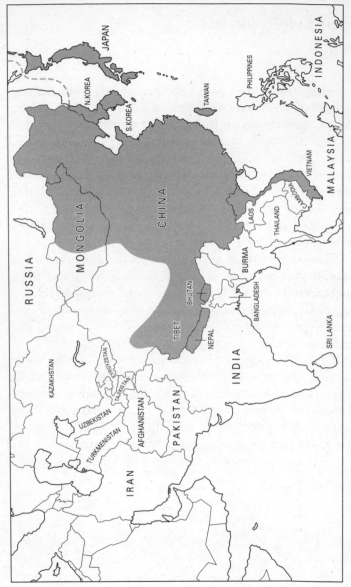

3. Mahāyāna Buddhism in Asia

Acknowledgements

In writing this book I have benefited greatly from the suggestions of students, colleagues, and friends. The students who took my course on Buddhism at Goldsmiths College in the session 1995–6 cheerfully acted as guinea pigs while I tested draft chapters. I can only hope that the experiment was not too painful. I have also benefited greatly from the cumulative knowledge of my colleagues Lance Cousins, Peter Harvey, and Charles Prebish, who were generous with their advice and steered me away from errors and oversights. Any that remain are my own responsibility.

A number of others also read parts or all of the manuscript. In particular I would like to thank Jo, who read everything carefully and made many astute and wise observations, and Ruth, who provided an objective perspective and reminded me how unlike our own the Buddhist world-view can seem.

Finally, it gives me great pleasure to thank George Miller of OUP for his advice, support, and encouragement in seeing this project through from inception to publication. My gratitude also to Rebecca Hunt for her skill in making the production process so smooth and efficient. No author could have wished for more professional editorial support.

DAMIEN KEOWN

Note on Citations

From time to time the reader will encounter references in the form D.ii.95. These are references to Buddhist scriptures, specifically the Pali Text Society editions of the early Buddhist canon. The key to the reference is as follows. The initial letter refers to one of the divisions (*nikāyas*) into which the Buddha's discourses (*suttas*) are collated.

D	*Dīgha Nikāya*
M	*Majjhima Nikāya*
A	*Aṅguttara Nikāya*
S	*Saṃyutta Nikāya*

The Roman numeral (ii) denotes the volume number, and the Arabic numeral (95) denotes the page number. Thus the reference D.ii.95 is to volume two, page 95, of the *Dīgha Nikāya*. A small number of references with the prefix *Vin* will also be encountered. These refer to a division of the Pali canon known as the *Vinaya* or Monastic Rule, which contains material relating to monastic life. Translations of the entire Pali canon have been published by the Pali Text Society. Other, more recent, translations are also available and are mentioned in the section on 'Further Reading' at the end.

Language and Pronunciation

Buddhist texts were composed in and translated into many languages including Pali, Sanskrit, Tibetan, Thai, Burmese, Chinese, Japanese, and Korean. The convention, however, is to cite Buddhist technical terms in either their Pali or Sanskrit forms. In this book I will generally use the Pali form, except where the Sanskrit form has become established in English usage, as in words such as 'karma' and 'nirvana'. Transliterated versions of proper names which are common in the secondary literature (e.g. Ashoka) will also be retained. Sanskrit and Pali equivalents for the most important terms will be shown in brackets.

Transliteration from Sanskrit and Pali requires the use of diacritics such as in the letters 'ā' and ṃ' seen above, since the twenty-six letters of the English alphabet are insufficient to represent the larger number of characters in Asian languages. A horizontal line (macron) above a vowel lengthens it, such that the character 'ā' is pronounced as in 'far' rather than 'fat'. For the most part the other marks do not affect pronunciation enough to be of any concern, with the following exceptions:

c   pronounced 'ch' as in 'choose'
ś or ṣ   pronounced 'sh' as in 'shoes'
ñ–   pronounced 'ny' as in Spanish 'mañana'

A dot beneath a consonant (ṭ, ḍ, etc.), indicates that the tongue touches the roof of the mouth when pronouncing these letters, to give the characteristic sound of English when spoken with an Indian accent.

1 Buddhism and Elephants

*T*he Buddha once told the story of the blind men and the elephant (*Udāna 69f.*). A former king of the town of Sāvatthi, he related, ordered all his blind subjects to be assembled and divided into groups. Each group was then taken to an elephant and introduced to a different part of the animal—the head, trunk, legs, tail, and so forth. Afterwards, the king asked each group to describe the nature of the beast. Those who had made contact with the head described an elephant as a water-pot; those familiar with the ears likened the animal to a winnowing-basket; those who had touched a leg said an elephant was like a post, and those who had felt a tusk insisted an elephant was shaped like a peg. The groups then fell to arguing amongst themselves each insisting its definition was correct and all the others were wrong.

The study of Buddhism over the past century or so has resembled the encounter of the blind men and the elephant in many ways. Students of Buddhism have tended to fasten onto a small part of the tradition and assume their conclusions held true about the whole. Often the parts they have seized on have been a little like the elephant's tusks—a striking, but unrepresentative, part of the whole animal. As a result, many erroneous and sweeping generalizations about

Buddhism have been made, such as that it is 'negative', 'world-denying', 'pessimistic', and so forth. Although this tendency to over-generalize is now less common, it is still found in some of the older literature where authors tended to exaggerate certain features of the tradition or assume that what was true of Buddhism in one culture or historical period held good everywhere.

The first lesson the story of the blind men teaches us, then, is that Buddhism is a large and complex subject, and we should be wary of generalizations made on the basis of familiarity with any single part. In particular, statements which begin 'Buddhists believe . . .' or 'Buddhism teaches . . .' must be treated with circumspection. We need to qualify them by asking *which* Buddhists are being referred to, *which* tradition of Buddhism they follow, *which* school or sect they belong to, and so forth, before these statements can be of much value. Some scholars would go further, and claim that the trans-cultural phenomenon known to the West as 'Buddhism' (the word 'Buddhism' only became established in Western usage in the 1830s) is not a single entity at all but a collection of sub-traditions. If so, perhaps we should speak of 'Buddhisms' (plural) rather than 'Buddhism' (singular). The tendency to 'deconstruct' Buddhism in this way, however, is probably best seen as a reaction to the earlier tendency to 'essentialize' it, in other words to assume that Buddhism was a monolithic institution which was everywhere the same. The middle way here is to think of Buddhism as resembling the elephant in the story: it has a curious assembly of somewhat unlikely parts but also a central bulk to which they are attached.

A second lesson we might learn from the story—one less obvious but no less important—is is that there are many kinds of blindness. Experiments in visual perception have shown that the mind has a great influence on what we see. To a large extent human beings see what they expect—or want—to see, and screen out material which does not fit their model of reality. In different cultures children are brought up to see and understand in different ways, which is why alien customs often seem curious or strange to outsiders but quite natural to members of the culture concerned. When dealing with other cultures, it is easy to project our own beliefs and values and then magically 'discover' them in the source material. Buddhism thus becomes exactly what we hoped (or feared) it would be. Even experts are not immune from anachronistically 'reading back' their own assumptions into the data, and many Western scholars have interpreted Buddhism in ways which clearly owe more to their own personal beliefs and upbringing than to Buddhism itself.

Apart from the susceptibility of individual perceptions to subjective influences of various kinds, there is also the risk of cultural stereotyping which arises in any encounter with 'the other'. Contemporary writers such as Edward Said have drawn attention to the West's tendency to construct in its art and literature an 'Orient' which is more a reflection of its own shadow-side than an accurate depiction of what is really there. There is no need to accept Said's elaborate conspiracy theory to the effect that the West stereotyped the Orient intellectually as a prelude to colonizing it politically to realize that in approaching the study of other cultures we cannot help but be influenced by residual attitudes and assumptions within our own culture of which we are barely conscious. In connection with the study of Buddhism, then, we must be alert to the risk of 'culture-blindness', and the misunderstandings which can arise from the assumption that Western categories and concepts apply to other cultures and civilizations.

Is Buddhism a Religion?

Problems of the kind just mentioned confront us as soon as we try we try to define what Buddhism is. Is it a religion? A philosophy? A way of life? A code of ethics? It is not easy to classify Buddhism as any of these things, and it challenges us to rethink some of these categories. What, for example, do we mean by 'religion'? Most people would say that religion has something to do with belief in God. God, in turn, is understood as a Supreme Being who created the world and the creatures in it. Furthermore, God takes a close interest (or at least has up to now) in the course of human history, by entering into covenants, making his will known in various ways, and intervening miraculously at critical junctures.

If belief in God in this sense is the essence of religion, then Buddhism cannot be a religion. Buddhism holds no such belief and, on the contrary, denies the existence of a creator god. In terms of the available Western categories, this would make Buddhism 'atheistic'. One problem with this designation, however, is that Buddhism recognizes the existence of supernatural beings such as gods and spirits. Another is that Buddhism seems not to have much in common with other atheistic ideologies such as Marxism. Perhaps, then, the categories of 'theistic' and 'atheistic' are not really appropriate here. Some have suggested that a new category—that of the 'non-theistic' religion—is needed to encompass Buddhism. Another possibility is that our original definition is simply too narrow. Could it be that the idea of a creator-God, while a central feature of one religion—or family of religions—is not the defining characteristic of all religions? While this notion is certainly central to the 'Abrahamic' or 'Semitic' religions, namely Judaism, Christianity, and Islam, there may be other systems of belief—such as Confucianism and Taoism—which resemble Western religion in many ways but lack this ingredient.

The Seven Dimensions of Religion

Since the discipline of comparative religion began in earnest in the post-war period, Buddhism has posed something of a puzzle for scholars who have attempted to provide a satisfactory definition of their subject. One of the most successful approaches to this problem is that adopted by Ninian Smart, who, rather than offer a definition, has analysed the phenomenon of religion into seven major dimensions. Thus religions may be said to have a practical and ritual dimension; an experiential and emotional dimension; a narrative or mythic dimension; a doctrinal and philosophical dimension; an ethical and legal dimension; a social and institutional dimension; and a material dimension. The attraction of this approach is that it does not reduce religion to any single doctrine or belief, or suggest that all religious believers have one thing in common. The data from different cultures and historical periods shows that generally they do not. Nevertheless, there seems to be a cluster of things which collectively give substance to the phenomenon we call 'religion'. How does Buddhism shape up in terms of these seven dimensions? Analysing it through each of them in turn should give us an advantage over the blind men in providing seven parts of the elephant to get hold of rather than one.

The Practical and Ritual Dimension

The practical or ritual dimension is less pronounced in Buddhism than in faiths of a strongly sacramental kind, such as Judaism and Orthodox Christianity. Nevertheless, Buddhism has rites and ceremonies of both a public and a private nature, many of which surround monastic life. Rituals of initiation are performed when a person becomes a monk (for example, the head is shaved), and there are periodic ceremonies such as the communal rehearsal of the monastic rules (the *pātimokkha*) on the days of the full moon and new moon each month. An important annual ceremony is the *kaṭhina* festival at which the laity offer new material for robes when the monks end their retreat for the rainy

A Religion without God?

Some scholars have denied that Buddhism is a religion because Buddhists do not believe in a Supreme Being or in a personal soul. But is this judgement based on too narrow a definition of 'religion'? According to Ninian Smart, religions have the following 'seven dimensions'. If Smart is correct, it seems justifiable to classify Buddhism as a religion.

1. Practical and Ritual
2. Experiential and Emotional
3. Narrative and Mythic
4. Doctrinal and Philosophical
5. Ethical and Legal
6. Social and Institutional
7. Material

season. Monks, however, do not normally perform sacramental rituals for the laity, and would not normally officiate at baptisms and marriages. These are thought of as family rituals rather than religious ones, although the participants may visit the temple later for a blessing. Buddhist monks have no priestly role—they are not intermediaries between God and mankind—and their ordination confers no supernatural powers or authority. Monks do attend funerals, however, since death is the gateway to an unseen world about which Buddhism has much to say. Buddhists also believe that the dying person's state of mind is particularly important in influencing the circumstances of the next rebirth.

There are wide variations in the liturgies of different Buddhist schools, and the influence of local traditions as well as demand from lay Buddhists (including those in the West) have combined to lead to the development of new ceremonies (a marriage ceremony, for example) to parallel those offered by other religions. The influence also works the other way round, and there are signs that certain Buddhist rituals—such as the *mizuko kuyō* rite which is performed in Japan following abortions—are being incorporated into some Western liturgies.

The Experiential and Emotional Dimension

The experiential and emotional dimension of Buddhism—Buddhism as a lived experience—is extremely important. The Buddha's personal experience of enlightenment is the bedrock of the entire Buddhist tradition. Time and again he invoked his own experience as authority for his doctrines, and suggested that teachings not validated by personal experience were of little value. The Buddha's enlightenment also included an emotional aspect in the form of a profound compassion which motivated him to propagate his teachings, or Dharma. Out of compassion for the suffering of mankind he spent the greater part of his life spreading a teaching which he realized was 'hard to see and understand, subtle, to be experienced by the wise', for the benefit of the few 'with little dust in their eyes who are wasting through not hearing it' (M.i.168).

The experiential dimension is of great importance because Buddhism regards the religious life as essentially a course in self-transformation. Spiritual exercises such as meditation generate altered states of consciousness that can accelerate spiritual development. In terms of its importance, meditation may be likened to prayer in Christianity, although Christian prayer and Buddhist meditation usually have different objectives: when Buddhists meditate, for example, they are not asking God to grant their wishes but endeavouring to cultivate wisdom and compassion.

This emphasis on the interior experiential dimension of religious practice links Buddhism with the mystical traditions of ancient India, such as yoga. In yoga, various exercises—such as control of the posture and breath—are used to gain control over body and mind and harness their latent powers. We will see in the next chapter that the Buddha experimented with some of these methods himself. These techniques are not unique to India and are found in other parts of the world. There are now signs of a revival of interest in the mystical dimension of Christianity, a development which has been triggered at least in part by the contemporary interest in Indian spirituality.

The Narrative and Mythic Dimension

Like other religions, Buddhism has its share of myths and legends. A 'myth' in this context does not mean something that is false: rather, myths are stories which have a compelling force by virtue of their ability to work simultaneously on several levels. They have a narrative content but also—like a parable—a metaphorical one which can be understood and interpreted in many ways. Freud, for example, thought that the myth of Oedipus—who killed his father and married his mother—contained important universal truths about human sexuality and the unconscious mind. Sometimes it is difficult to know whether the content of a myth is to be taken at face value or not. Those who believe in the literal truth of the Bible will tend to read the story of creation in Genesis as a factual account of how the world began. Others may prefer the scientific version of events while accepting that the Genesis account reveals a profound truth about the relationship between God and the universe. Early Buddhism has its own 'creation myth' in the *Aggañña Sutta*, and there are many popular narratives such as the *Jātaka* stories, a collection of moral tales about the Buddha's previous lives. In some of these tales the characters are animals, not unlike Aesop's Fables, and at the end the Buddha reveals that he himself was the principal character in a former life.

Many dramatic episodes involving the supernatural enliven Buddhist literature, becoming more exaggerated and elaborate as the centuries pass. Even in the earliest sources gods and spirits make frequent appearances. They are commonly depicted in Buddhist art and literature as forming part of the audience at significant episodes in the Buddha's life. One vivid narrative recounts how just prior to his enlightenment the Buddha did battle with Māra, the Evil One, winning a great victory and scattering his legions. There are also more mundane narratives and chronicles which recount the history of Buddhism in various cultures, although these too contain their fantastic elements.

The Doctrinal and Philosophical Dimension

Buddhists in Asia do not use the term 'Buddhism' to describe their religion and refer to it as either the Dharma ('Law') or the *Buddha-sāsana* ('teachings of the Buddha'). Some would be unhappy about the application of the term 'doctrine' to their beliefs, seeing this as having overtones associated with Western religion. However, if by 'doctrine' we understand the systematic formulation of religious teachings in an intellectually coherent form, it does not seem unreasonable to apply it to Buddhism. The core doctrinal teachings are contained in a set of interlinked propositions known as the Four Noble Truths, which were formulated by the founder. The task of studying, clarifying, and expounding doctrines is typically the responsibility of a literate, educated élite. In Buddhism, the custody of the texts and their interpretation is the responsibility of the *Saṅgha*, or Order of monks. Not all monks, however, are philosophers, and within the Buddhist tradition there have been those who have felt that mystical experience—of the kind gained through meditation—was a surer path to liberation than the study of texts. In spite of this, Buddhism down the centuries has invested enormous intellectual energy in scholarship, as can be seen from the voluminous texts and treatises preserved in many Asian languages. Only a small percentage of this literature has so far been translated, although many of the most important scriptures are now available in English or other European languages.

The Ethical and Legal Dimension

Buddhism is widely respected as one of the world's most ethical religions. At the heart of Buddhist ethics is the principle of non-harming (*ahiṃsā*), which manifests itself in the respect for life for which Buddhism is renowned. Buddhists have a scrupulous respect for all living creatures, whether human or animal, and regard the intentional destruction of life as a grave wrong. This philosophy has led many (though by no means all) Buddhists to become vegetarians and to adopt pacifism as a way of life. The principle of non-harming also takes on a positive role in the practical contribution made by Buddhist monks and laity in founding hospitals, hospices, schools, and charitable institutions of many kinds.

Violence of any kind is abhorrent to most Buddhists, and the use of force to further the aims of religion—for example in the form of a crusade or *jihad*—seems incomprehensible. This is not to say that the Buddhist record is entirely spotless, and there have been episodes in Asian history where Buddhism has been exploited for political purposes and used to justify military campaigns. However, there has been little to compare to the crusades and religious wars in medieval and early-modern Europe. This century, Tibetan Buddhists have adopted a policy of peaceful resistance to the invasion of their country by the Chinese in 1950, in the aftermath of which it is estimated a million Tibetans died and 6,000 monasteries were destroyed. Serious abuses of human rights have continued ever since.

The five dimensions described thus far are all of an abstract nature. The final two concern religion as embodied in social and physical form.

The Social and Institutional Dimension

Alfred North Whitehead defined religion as 'what a man does with his solitariness', but there is more to religion than private interior experience (in terms of our present framework, we can see that this definition places too much emphasis on the experiential dimension). Religious believers commonly feel themselves to be part of a community, and have often seen this as having a political as well as religious significance, as in the medieval concept of 'Christendom'. Such a perspective is also apparent in Islam, which regards religious law as holding sway over all aspects of public and private life.

The social nucleus of Buddhism is the order of monks and nuns (*Saṅgha*) founded by the Buddha. While the Buddhist Order is the central social institution, however, Buddhism is not just a religion for monks. Early sources offer a sociological classification of Buddhism as 'The Fourfold Order', consisting of monks, nuns, and devout male and female lay disciples (*upāsaka/upāsikā*). The emphasis here is on inclusivity and interdependence, both with respect to gender and the lay and monastic estates. While a clear distinction exists between monastics and laity in much of the Buddhist world, there have also been attempts to blur or remove the boundaries between the two, a tendency which has met with the greatest success in Japan.

The social organization of a religion can take many forms, from small groups led by individual teachers to large hierarchically structured institutions with millions of adherents. Many permutations are found in Buddhism. The Buddha was originally a wandering teacher who attracted followers

Buddhist Sects and Schools

Over the centuries, many sects and schools of Buddhism have developed. A major division is between the conservative Buddhism of south Asia found in countries such as Sri Lanka, Burma, and Thailand, and the more doctrinally innovative schools of the north encountered in Tibet, central Asia, China, and Japan. In south Asia the Theravāda school predominates. Its name means the 'Abiding Teaching', or 'Original Teaching', although it is commonly translated as the 'Doctrine of the Elders'. This school regards itself as the custodian of the authentic early teachings which date back to the Buddha himself. The schools of north Asia belong to the movement known as the Mahāyāna, meaning the 'Great Vehicle'. Individual Buddhists would identify themselves as belonging to one or other of these two 'families', in a way that Muslims would regard themselves as Sunni or Shiite, or Western Christians would think of themselves as either Protestant or Catholic.

through his personal charisma. As their numbers grew, an institutional infrastructure developed in the form of a monastic community with rules and regulations. The Buddha, however, stated that he did not regard himself as the leader of this community and declined to appoint a successor when he died. Instead, he encouraged his followers to live according to his teachings (the Dharma) and the Monastic Rule, and be 'lamps (or islands) unto yourselves' (D.ii.100). While different countries today have their ecclesiastical authorities, Buddhism has never had a single head and there has been no central office corresponding to that of the Pope in Christianity. Given the absence of central authority, Buddhism has tended to fissure readily when disagreements arose over matters of doctrine and practice. Buddhist chronicles speak of eighteen schools existing within a couple of centuries of the Buddha's death, and many more have arisen since then.

In terms of social organization the Buddha seems to have preferred a republican model of the kind in use among his own people. He encouraged monks to hold 'full and frequent assemblies' (D.ii.76) and to take decisions on the basis of consensus. The social organization of Buddhism varies from one culture to another, and it has demonstrated great flexibility in adapting to the traditions of the indigenous cultures with which it came into contact. As it spreads in the West, it is to be expected that democratic forms of social organization will evolve as Buddhist communities develop social structures appropriate to their needs.

The Material Dimension

The seventh and final dimension is to a large extent derivative from the social one. The material dimension includes objects in which the spirit of a religion becomes incarnate, such as churches, temples, works of art, statues, sacred sites, and holy places like pilgrimage sites. In India, various sites connected with the Buddha's life have become important centres of pilgrimage, such as the place of his birth, his enlightenment, and the park where he gave his first sermon. Elsewhere in Asia there are numerous Buddhist sites of archaeological, historical, and legendary significance. These include huge rock carvings, such as those at Polunnaruwa in Sri Lanka (see p. 89), Bamiyan in Afghanistan, and Yün-Kang in China. The most common reminder of the presence of Buddhism in Asia, however, is the ubiquitous *stūpa*, a dome-shaped monument which under the influence of east Asian architectural styles evolved into the pagoda.

Another artefact of great importance in Buddhism is the text. Religious scriptures are treated with great respect since they contain the teachings of the Buddha and embody his wisdom. To copy, recite, or memorize texts is regarded as a pious activity, as is the work of translating them into different languages.

Summary

We can see from the above that religion is a complex phenomenon to which no simple dictionary-style definition can do justice, especially not one distilled pre-eminently from the religious experience of the West. Once we begin to think of a religion as an organism with various dimensions, however, it becomes easier to see how Buddhism—despite its unusual and distinctive features—can take its place among the family of world religions. Returning to our original question, we can also see why it would be inadequate to define Buddhism simply as a philosophy, a way of life, or a code of ethics. It includes all of these things and sometimes seems to present itself predominantly in one of these modes. However, this depends largely on the perspective from which it is being viewed, and the extent to which some of its dimensions are being ignored. If someone wishes to see Buddhism as a rational philosophy free of religious superstition, then—by focusing on the doctrinal and philosophical dimension—it can be understood in this way. If another wishes to see it essentially as a quest for mystical experience, then—by making the experiential dimension central—that too is possible. Finally, someone who wishes to see Buddhism as a set of humanistic moral values will also find justification for that view by making the ethical and legal dimension primary.

I have mentioned these particular interpretations of Buddhism because they are ones which have proved popular with Westerners in the course of the last century. While not altogether illegitimate, they suffer from being incomplete, and typically represent a reaction of some kind to the perceived deficiencies of religion in the West. To focus on just one of the dimensions of Buddhism in this way is to make the same mistake as the blind men did in grasping hold of just one part of the elephant.

Having concluded that Buddhism is a religion, our task in the following chapters is to explore some of its dimensions in more detail. The ones which will receive most attention in this book are the doctrinal, experiential, and ethical dimensions, although reference will be made to others at appropriate points. First, however, we must learn something about the life of the founder of Buddhism, Siddhattha Gotama.

2 The Buddha

*T*he Buddha was born in the Terai lowlands near the foothills of the Himalayas just inside the borders of modern-day Nepal. His people were known as the Sakyas and for this reason the Buddha is sometimes referred to as Sakyamuni or 'the sage of the Sakyas'. To his followers he is known as the *Bhagavat* or 'Lord'. 'Buddha' is a not a personal name but an honorific title which means 'awakened one'. Although strictly speaking the title can only be used of someone after he has attained enlightenment, I will use it here to refer to the Buddha in the earlier part of his life as well. The Buddha's personal name, as noted above, was Siddhattha Gotama (Sanskrit: Siddhartha Gautama).

The conventional dates for the Buddha's life are 566–486 BC, although more recent research indicates that some time around 410 BC would be a more likely date for his death (chronology at this period is only accurate to within ten years). The traditional sources suggest that the Buddha and his kin belonged to the second of the four Indian castes—the aristocratic warrior caste known as the *khattiyas* (Sanskrit: *kṣatriyas*), although there is no other evidence that the caste system was current among the Sakya people.

References to the royal status of the Buddha's father,

Early Scriptures

The teachings of the Buddha are recorded in various collections of scripture known as 'canons'. These derive from an oral tradition which goes back to the time of the Buddha, and which was preserved through a method of communal chanting. The only one of these early canons which has been preserved intact is the Pali Canon, so-called because it is written in Pali, a vernacular language related to Sanskrit and close to that spoken by the Buddha. The Pali Canon was committed to writing in Sri Lanka around the middle of the first century BC and consists of three divisions or 'baskets' (*piṭaka*). These are (1) the Discourses (*Sutta Piṭaka*) or sermons of the Buddha, which are subdivided into five divisions known as *nikāyas*; (2) the Monastic Rule (*Vinaya Piṭaka*), which contains the rules of monastic discipline; and (3) the Scholastic Treatises (*Abhidhamma Piṭaka*), a slightly later compilation of scholastic works.

Suddhodana, and to the pomp and ceremony of his court, as found particularly in later texts, are most likely an exaggeration. Nevertheless, the Buddha's noble birth and high status are popular themes in Buddhist art and literature, and his aristocratic background—although perhaps not quite as lofty as the sources would have us believe—undoubtedly helped him make a favourable impression at the courts of north-east India which he visited as a wandering teacher.

A certain amount of information is preserved in the Pali canon (*see text box*) about the Buddha's life, but no attempt was made to piece the details together into a continuous narrative until about five hundred years after his death. Earlier, within a couple of centuries of his passing, partial accounts of his life began to appear, suggesting increasing curiosity about the life of this remarkable man. The most famous and elegant account of the Buddha's life is an epic poem known as the *Buddhacarita* or 'Acts of the Buddha', composed in the first century AD by the famous Buddhist literary figure Aśvaghoṣa. By this time the early biographical fragments had become embellished with fanciful details which makes it difficult to separate fact from legend. These narrative accounts of the Buddha's life may have inspired the creation of images of the Buddha, which are not found until around the second century AD. Before then he was represented in art only through symbols, such as a tree, a wheel, or a parasol, either out of respect or because of the difficulty of giving aesthetic expression to the transcendent state he had attained. In due course, however, artists began to create representations of the Buddha in stone and other media and these became the focus of popular devotion.

The Life of the Buddha

The information about the Buddha's life found in the earliest sources is fragmentary. Sometimes when teaching on a subject, the Buddha recalled an episode from his early life which he then proceeded to narrate. Some of these biographical fragments are detailed while others are vague, and the chronology of the episodes is not always clear. For reasons of this kind, producing a biography of the Buddha based on the extant sources is no easy task. The concept of a biography, furthermore, is a comparatively recent Western invention, and biography did not exist as a literary genre in ancient India. Similar difficulties have beset attempts to construct biographies of other early religious figures such as Jesus, and it is unlikely that a quest for the 'historical Buddha' would meet with any greater success. An added complication is that since Buddhists believe in reincarnation, a complete biography of the Buddha would need to include his previous lives!

Although there is no early continuous narrative of the Buddha's life, there is general agreement on the relative chronology of certain key episodes in his career. In a nut-shell, the facts are as follows. He was married at 16 to Yaśodharā who subsequently bore him a son named Rāhula ('Fetter'). Shortly after the birth of his son the Buddha left home at the age of 29 to seek religious knowledge, and attained enlightenment at the age of 35. The remaining forty-five years of his life were spent giving religious teachings and he died at the age of 80. Buddhists traditionally focus on certain key events in the Buddha's career as the most important, and commemorate them in various ways in literature, myth and ritual, and pilgrimage to the sites where they took place. The four most important events are his birth, enlightenment, first sermon, and death.

Birth

The Buddha's birth, not unlike the birth of Jesus, is said to have been surrounded by miraculous events. Later texts describe how the Buddha was conceived when his mother Māyā dreamed that a white baby elephant entered her side. This incident is depicted in the relief on p. 20. The dream was interpreted to mean that she would bear a son who would be either a great emperor (*cakkavatti*) or a great religious teacher. As was the custom when a pregnancy approached its term, Māyā embarked on a journey from Kapilavatthu, the capital of the Sakyan republic, to the home of her rela-tives to give birth. As the queen and her escort reached a delightful grove at Lumbinī she went into labour and gave birth standing up holding on to the trunk of a Sal tree. It is reported that the denizens of the heavens arrived to marvel at this great event, for the birth of a Buddha is a joyous and momentous occasion. The earth shook and the gods laid the child upon the ground where it was bathed in a miraculous shower of water. Immediately the infant stood up, took seven steps and declared that this would be the last time he would

1. *The Buddha's Conception*: The Buddha's mother, Queen Māyā, dreams that the future Buddha enters her side in the form of a white baby elephant, a very auspicious symbol. Detail from a Tibetan *'thangka*

be born. The boy was named Siddhattha Gotama. Siddhattha means 'one who has achieved his aim' and Gotama is a clan name deriving from the name of an ancient Indian sage. Just seven days after the birth the Buddha's mother died, and the child was raised by his mother's sister, Pajāpatī, who became Suddhodana's second wife.

Little detail is provided in the Pali Canon about the Buddha's childhood, but the impression is created that he lived a life of luxury within the walls of his father's three palaces, one reserved for each of the three seasons of the Indian year. The young man wore fine garments, was perfumed with fragrances and surrounded by musicians and attendants who ministered to his every need. Although these conditions might be calculated to produce the archetypal 'spoilt child' the Buddha's character does not seem to have suffered unduly, and he is depicted as a precocious but considerate child with a keen intelligence and latent psychic powers.

The Four Signs

Although palace life was comfortable it was unfulfilling, and the Buddha yearned for a deeper and more spiritually satisfying way of life. The later legends represent this disaffection in a story in which the Buddha makes four visits outside the palace in a chariot. His over-protective father—constantly fearful that his son would leave home to fulfil his destiny as a religious teacher as predicted in Māyā's dream—arranged for the streets to be filled with healthy smiling people so that Siddhattha would not be troubled by the sight of any unpleasantness. All aged and infirm people were removed from the route, but by chance—or as later sources have it, the intervention of the gods—the Buddha encountered an old man. He was thunderstruck by the discovery of old age and ordered his charioteer to return immediately to the palace where he reflected upon what it meant to grow old. In the second journey he encountered a sick man and in the third a corpse being carried to the cremation ground. These experiences impressed upon him above all the transient nature of human existence and he realized that not even the palace walls could keep suffering and death at bay. On the fourth trip outside the Buddha encountered a religious mendicant (*samaṇa*) and was inspired by the thought that he himself might seek a spiritual solution to the problems of the human condition. That very night he decided to leave the palace, and, taking a last look at his sleeping wife and child, departed to become a homeless mendicant.

This simple, poignant story is unlikely to be true in the literal sense. It is hard to believe that the Buddha was as naïve as the story portrays him, or that his disenchantment with palace life was nearly as sudden. It might be more useful to read the story as a parable in which palace life represents complacency and self-delusion, and the vision of the four signs the dawning of a realization about the nature of human life. If the Buddha were alive today he would see the four signs all around: every elderly person, every hospital, and every funeral would bespeak the brevity and fragility of life, while every church and religious minister would be testimony to the belief that a religious solution to these problems can be found. The parable seems to suggest that although the signs are all around, most people—like the young Buddha—construct mental barriers (the palace walls) to keep unpleasant realities at bay. Even then, there are times when the unwelcome facts of life thrust themselves upon us in a manner it is impossible to ignore, such as in sickness or bereavement, just as they did when the Buddha went forth in his chariot.

Renunciation and Austerities

Shaken from his complacency the Buddha made the radical decision to turn his back on family life and go in search of spiritual knowledge. This decision was not unprecedented in India, and the *Samaṇa* movement—a counter-culture of homeless religious mendicants—was already well established by the Buddha's time. Many people had made a similar choice to renounce the world, and the Buddha became yet another recruit to these bands of wandering seekers and philosophers.

The Buddha's first teacher, a man by the name of Āḷāra Kālāma, taught him a meditational technique which induced a profound state of trance. The Buddha was a good student, and quickly mastered the ability to enter and abide in a state of absorption known as 'the sphere of nothingness'. So quickly and thoroughly did the Buddha master this technique that Āḷāra offered him joint leadership of the group. The Buddha refused, since, although the experience was serene and blissful, it was not the permanent solution he sought; eventually one exited the state and came back to normal waking consciousness with the fundamental problems of birth, sickness, old age, and death still unresolved.

The Buddha continued his quest and studied next under another teacher by the name of Uddaka Rāmaputta. Uddaka taught the Buddha a more sophisticated technique which allowed the practitioner to enter 'the sphere of neither perception nor non-perception', an even more sublime state of mind in which consciousness itself seemed almost to disappear. Uddaka was so impressed with his student that he offered to become the Buddha's disciple, but the Buddha refused, feeling that the ability to attain mystical states of consciousness was good and valuable as far as it went but was not the goal he sought.

After these experiments with meditation the Buddha turned his attention to techniques of a different kind. These involved extreme austerities, the aim of which was to subdue the appetites and passions. First the Buddha practised an exercise in breath control, which involved retaining the breath for longer and longer periods of time. Rather than producing spiritual knowledge, however, all this resulted in was painful headaches. Abandoning this technique, the Buddha tried a second method which involved reducing his intake of food to minuscule proportions, just a spoonful of bean soup a day. Before long he became emaciated, was unable to sit upright, and his hair began to fall out. It became clear to him that this form of self-mortification was not producing results either, so he abandoned it. The Buddha's exertions, however, were not entirely wasted, for his experience had now taught him that extremes of any kind were unproductive. His earlier life of self-indulgence had been unsatisfying, as was his six-year experiment with ascetic penances. He came to see that the most productive course was a 'middle way' between extremes of this kind. The most appropriate lifestyle, accordingly, would be one of moderation in which the appetites were neither denied nor indulged to excess.

The Enlightenment

Acting on this principle the Buddha once again began to take food and returned to the practice of meditation. He now made rapid progress and in the course of one night seated beneath a large tree, later known as the Bodhi tree (*ficus religiosus*), attained the complete state of awakening which he sought. During the first watch of the night he acquired the power to look back through his previous existences, recalling them in full detail. In the second watch of the night he attained the clairvoyant power which allowed him to see the decease and rebirth of all types of beings in the universe according to their good and bad deeds. During the third watch he attained the knowledge that his spiritual defilements had been eliminated and that he had rooted out craving and ignorance once and for all. He had 'done what

2. *The Buddha gains enlightenment*: The Buddha is depicted here in the lotus posture just after he gained enlightenment. He called upon the Earth to witness his achievement by touching it with his right hand. Western Tibet, 11th–12th cent. AD

needed to be done'—attained nirvana and put an end to rebirth, just as he prophesied he would when he was born.

The place the Buddha attained enlightenment was known as Bodh Gayā, and the Buddha remained there for seven weeks pondering his future. He wondered whether he should become a religious teacher but was deterred by the difficulty of communicating the profound realization he had attained. For a time he inclined towards a life of privacy and seclusion, but following an appeal from one of the gods (Buddhism has a rich pantheon of gods who are somewhat like angels in Christianity) he was moved by compassion and decided to proclaim his teachings—or Dharma (Pali: *Dhamma*)—to the world. Realizing through his psychic powers that his two former teachers had died, the Buddha set out for Benares on the Ganges where he knew he would find a group of five former associates who had earlier turned their back on him when he rejected the path of austerities.

First Sermon and Teaching Career

Arriving in a park set aside for royal deer near Benares the Buddha was, after some initial hesitation, welcomed by his former colleagues who quickly realized the transformation which had taken place in him. The Buddha proclaimed himself a *Tathāgata* ('one who has attained what is really so') and preached his first sermon, a momentous event in the history of Buddhism. The first sermon is preserved as a discourse (*sutta*) called *Setting in Motion the Wheel of the Dharma*. It

---

3. *The First Sermon*: The Buddha makes the gesture (*mudrā*) of the wheel, symbolizing the First Sermon, known as 'Setting in Motion the Wheel of the Dharma'. The plinth shows the wheel of the Dharma in the centre, with deer on each side symbolizing the Deer Park near Benares where the sermon was given. Sarnath Museum, Gupta period

contains the essential teachings of Buddhism set out in a for-mula known as the Four Noble Truths, which will be dis-cussed in more detail in Chapter Four. The wheel is an important symbol in Buddhism, and is often used to repre-sent the Dharma. The First Sermon was the event which gave initial impetus to the wheel of the Dharma, a wheel which would roll forward unceasingly as Buddhism spread throughout Asia.

On hearing the First Sermon one member of the audience immediately glimpsed the truth and became a 'stream-enterer' or one who has achieved the preliminary degree of spiritual understanding. As the Buddha expounded his teachings further the remaining four mendicants also achieved this state. All five became his disciples and were ordained as monks (*bhikkhu*) in a simple ceremony. On hear-ing the Buddha's second sermon the five attained full enlight-enment. They and others like them were known as Arhats (saints) rather than Buddhas, since the term Buddha is reserved for a person who discovers the way to enlighten-ment by himself rather than hearing it from another.

The teachings spread quickly and soon a large number of people had gained enlightenment. The early texts speak of a body of sixty Arhats, whom the Buddha charged to go forth as missionaries and spread the teachings out of compassion for the world. After five years when the order of monks had become established, the Buddha was prevailed upon to institute an equivalent order for nuns. Although initially reluctant—monasticism itself was a new development and an order of nuns something almost unprecedented—the Buddha eventually agreed. The order of nuns did not flour-ish to the same degree as the male order, and in general today the *Saṅgha* denotes essentially the order of monks.

Little biographical detail is available concerning the latter half of the Buddha's life. It is clear, however, that his time was taken up travelling on foot through the towns and villages of north-east India addressing audiences of many kinds from different religious, social, and economic backgrounds. His journeys took him over a territory some 150 miles long by 250 miles wide, an area somewhat smaller than Ireland or the state of Pennsylvania. The Buddha is often depicted holding audiences in the course of which he gives teachings, answers questions, and engages in debate with people from all walks of life. His manner was always courteous and calm, and the numerous converts mentioned in the texts bear witness to his powers of persuasion and personal charisma. Occasionally he is depicted as working miracles, an ability attributed to the psychic powers he developed through the practice of meditation. As his popularity increased and the numbers of his followers swelled, residential centres became established at which monks would remain for part of the year, notably during the rainy season when travel was difficult. Often these residences were donated to the Order by kings or wealthy patrons, and in due course they evolved into permanent institutions known as *vihāras* or monasteries.

Death

An important text known as *The Discourse of the Great Decease* provides an account of the events in the few months leading up to the Buddha's death. By now the Buddha was 80 and in failing health, but continued his travels on foot as he had done throughout his life, relying on his mental powers to suppress the effects of his infirmity. At this point important decisions about the future arose. Would he appoint a successor? Who would lead the Order after he was gone? In conversation with Ānanda, his cousin and loyal personal attendant, the Buddha stated there was no need for a successor since he had never regarded himself as the 'leader' of the Order. Instead, the Dharma should be the guide after he was gone, and monks should hold fast to this and the *Vinaya*, the code of rules he had laid down for the regulation of monastic life. Furthermore, he advised that each person should think for himself on matters of doctrine, cross-referencing views and opinions against the scriptures before deciding whether to accept them. In keeping with the Buddha's advice, there never arose a central source of authority in Buddhism on matters of doctrine, and no institution or body is authorized to promulgate dogmas and creeds for the religion as a whole.

The Buddha died at a small town called Kusinārā, lying on his right side between two Sal trees, which, the texts report, miraculously bloomed out of season. Although it is often said that he died from food poisoning after eating a meal of pork donated by a lay follower, it is clear from the account in the *Discourse of the Great Decease* that he recovered from this and his death occurred somewhat later, apparently due to natural causes. He instructed that his remains should be cremated and treated like those of a great king (*cakkavatti*) by being enshrined in a bell-shaped monument known as a *stūpa* (Pali: *thūpa*) which could be used as a site for offerings and devotion. Shortly before his death the Buddha called the monks together and gave them an opportunity to ask final questions. None were forthcoming, which suggests by this time his teachings were fully explained and well understood amongst his followers. The Buddha then uttered his last words: 'Decay is inherent in all things: be sure to strive with clarity of mind (for nirvana).' Serene and self-composed he then passed through several levels of meditative trance (*jhāna*) before entering final nirvana.

3 Karma and Rebirth

*T*he texts report that on the night of his enlightenment the Buddha gained the ability to recall his previous lives. It is said that he remembered not just one or two, but a vast number, together with the details of what his name, caste, profession, and so forth had been in each life. Elsewhere the Buddha states that he could remember back 'as far as ninety-one eons' (M.i.483), one eon being roughly equal to the lifespan of a galaxy. Although Buddhist doctrine holds that neither the beginning of the process of cyclic rebirth nor its end can ever be known with certainty, it is clear that the number of times a person may be reborn is almost infinite. This process of repeated rebirth is known as *saṃsāra* or 'endless wandering', a term suggesting continuous movement like the flow of a river. All living creatures are part of this cyclic movement and will continue to be reborn until they attain nirvana.

The idea of reincarnation did not originate with Buddhism and had existed in India for several centuries before the Buddha's time. The belief is common to many cultures and was widespread in the classical West before coming to be seen as incompatible with Christian doctrine around the sixth century. Indian conceptions about rebirth are distinctive, however, because of their association with the doctrine of karma, which holds that the circumstances of future rebirths are determined by the moral deeds a person performs in this life. Karma (Pali: *kamma*) is of fundamental importance to Buddhist thought, and to understand it we must explore a cluster of related concepts concerning cosmology and time.

The Buddhist Universe

Buddhist thought divides the universe into two categories: the physical universe, which is thought of as a receptacle or 'container' (*bhājana*), and the 'beings' (*sattva*) or life-forms which reside in it. The physical universe is formed by the interaction of the five elements, namely earth, water, fire, air, and space (*ākāśa*). The last of these, space—thought of as infinite—is regarded in Indian thought not simply as the absence of the other four but an element in its own right. Through the interaction of the five elements there evolve 'world-systems' (roughly equivalent to the modern concept of a galaxy) which are found throughout the six directions of the universe (north, south, east, west, above, and below).

These world-systems are thought to undergo cycles of evolution and decline lasting billions of years. They come into being, endure for a time, and then slowly disintegrate before being destroyed in a great cataclysm. In due course they evolve again to complete a vast cycle known as a 'great eon'. Naturally, the beings who inhabit the physical universes are not unaffected by these events, and indeed there is some suggestion that it is the moral status of the inhabitants that determines the fate of the world-system. A world inhabited by ignorant and selfish people, for example, would decline at a faster speed than one with a wise and virtuous population. This notion that beings are not just the caretakers of their environment, but in some sense create it, has important implications for Buddhist thinking on ecology.

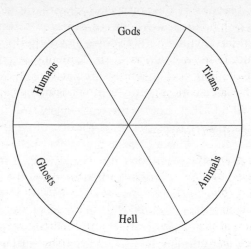

The 'Wheel of Life' (bhavacakra) or Six Realms of Rebirth

It will already be clear that Buddhist cosmology differs in important respects from religious thinking in the West. In the Book of Genesis creation is depicted as a unique event, and the Bible teaches that the world will end on the Day of Judgement. Between these two events a temporary window of time has opened in eternity within which a unique drama—that of the Fall and Redemption—is played out. It is this drama that constitutes 'history', conceived of as a linear and generally forward-moving sequence of events. In this drama (the secular version of which substitutes 'progress' for redemption), human affairs are always centre stage. Nowhere is this seen more clearly than in pre-Copernican cosmology which locates the earth at the very centre of the universe. From an Indian perspective, however, this world-picture is anthropocentric and parochial. The earth is far from being the hub around which the cosmos revolves, and humans are not the only actors on the stage. Time, moreover, is conceived of as cyclic rather than linear: history has no overall direction or purpose, and similar patterns of events may repeat themselves many times over.

A Buddhist creation myth found in the *Aggañña Sutta* tells a quite different story from the Book of Genesis. The myth describes how the inhabitants of a world-system which has been destroyed are gradually reborn within a new one that is evolving. At first their bodies are translucent and there is no distinction between the sexes. As the fabric of the new world-system becomes denser, these spirit-like beings become attracted to it and begin to consume it like food. Slowly, their bodies become less ethereal until they resemble the gross physical bodies we have now. Competition for food leads to quarrels and disputes, and the people elect a king to keep the peace, an event which marks the origins of social life. Although the myth may be intended as much as a satire on human society as an account of creation, it provides an interesting contrast with the Book of Genesis: whereas the Judaeo-Christian tradition attributes the Fall of Man to pride and disobedience, Buddhism locates the origin of human suffering in desire.

The Six Realms of Rebirth

Within a world-system there are various 'realms' of rebirth. Early sources list five, but later ones add a further realm—that of the Titans—making six in all, and this is the scheme I will adopt here. The six realms are a popular theme in Buddhist art and are often depicted in the 'wheel of life' (*bhavacakra*). This can be seen in diagrammatic form on p. 33. The three realms below the centre line are regarded as particularly unfortunate. In a sense the arrangement is like an expanded version of the traditional Christian scheme of hell, purgatory, earth, and heaven, with the difference that a person can transmigrate repeatedly from one realm to another. The Buddhist heaven, shown at the top, is subdivided by later sources (post-fifth century) into twenty-six different levels or 'mansions', so when the other five realms are included a total of thirty-one possible rebirth-destinations is arrived at.

The easiest way to picture this arrangement is to think of an office block with thirty-one floors. At the bottom is hell— a place of woe where beings suffer the results of evil acts done in previous lives. While in hell they are subject to various torments—often depicted vividly in popular art—such as being boiled in oil or hacked limb from limb. The Buddhist hell (strictly 'hells', since there are many of them), however, is unlike the Christian one in two respects. The first is that it is not a place of final damnation: in this respect it corresponds more to the Christian purgatory, a temporary state from which a person will eventually be released. Release comes when the evil karma that sent one to hell has run its course. The second difference is that in Buddhism there are both hot hells and cold hells; in the latter the suffering is due to freezing rather than roasting.

Above hell is the animal realm. Rebirth as an animal is undesirable for obvious reasons. Animals are governed by brute instinct and lack the intellectual capacity to understand the nature of their situation or do much to improve it. They are also hunted for food by human and other predators. Above the animals is the realm of ghosts. These are unhappy spirits that hover around the fringes of the human world and can sometimes be glimpsed as shadowy forms. For the most part, ghosts are former human beings who developed strong attachments which keep them bound to the earth. They are consumed by desires they can never satisfy, and are depicted in popular art as wraith-like creatures with large stomachs and tiny mouths symbolizing their insatiable yet constantly unsatisfied hunger. The fourth level is that of the Titans, a race of demonic warlike beings at the mercy of violent impulses. Motivated by a lust for power they constantly seek conquests in which they find no fulfilment.

On the fifth level is the human world. Rebirth as a human being is regarded as both highly desirable and difficult to attain. Although there are many higher levels on which rebirth can be achieved, they are potentially a handicap to spiritual progress. By being reborn as a god in an idyllic paradise one can easily become complacent and lose sight of the need to strive for nirvana. Human existence, by contrast, offers constant reminders of the vagaries of life (for example the 'four signs' seen by the Buddha such as old age and sickness) as well as the opportunity to seek a permanent solution to life's problems. Human beings have reason and free will, and can use these to understand the Dharma and implement Buddhist teachings. Life as a human being is thus seen as the 'middle way' in offering an appropriate balance between pleasure and suffering.

The twenty-six upper storeys of our building (levels 6–31) are the abodes or mansions of the gods. The top five heavens (levels 23–27) are known as the 'Pure Abodes', and can only be attained by those known as 'non-returners'. These are beings on the point of gaining enlightenment who will not be reborn again as human beings. The gods below these levels (*deva*) are simply beings who, due to the performance of good deeds, enjoy harmonious and blissful states of existence. Nevertheless, they are subject to karma and are reborn like everyone else. The upper levels of the heavens are increasingly sublime, and the lifespan of the gods increases at each stage, extending to billions of years measured in human time. Time, however, is relative and is perceived differently by different beings; a human lifetime, for example, seems like a day to the gods at the lower levels.

The Three Spheres

The notion of the six realms and thirty-one levels overlaps with another conception of the universe as divided into three

4. *The Buddhist Universe*: The circle in the middle represents
the flat surface of the earth which was thought to support four
large continents of different shapes. Above this are the heavenly
mansions inhabited by the gods, and below the hells and other
realms of suffering. Thailand, AD *c.* 1820

Level		Meditation Level (*jhāna*)	
31	Neither perception nor non-perception	8	Sphere of Formlessness (*arūpāvacara*)
30	Nothingness	7	
29	Infinite Consciousness	6	
28	Infinite Space	5	
27 12	Higher Gods	4 3 2 1	Sphere of pure Form (*rūpāvacara*)
11 . 6	Lower Gods		Sphere of Sense-desires (*kāmāvacara*)
5	Humans		
4	Titans		
3	Ghosts		
2	Animals		
1	Hell		

Diagram of the Buddhist Universe

spheres. The lowest of these is the 'sphere of sense-desires' (*kāmāvacara*) which includes all of the levels up to the sixth heaven above the human world. Next is the 'sphere of pure form' (*rūpāvacara*), a rarefied spiritual state in which the gods perceive and communicate by a kind of telepathy. This extends up to level twenty-seven. Highest of all is the 'sphere of formlessness' (*arūpāvacara*), an almost indescribably sublime state beyond all shape and form in which beings exist as pure mental energy.

The gods in the four levels of the sphere of formlessness apprehend phenomena in four increasingly subtle ways: in the lowest (level 28) as infinite space, in the second (level 29) as infinite consciousness, and in the third (level 30) as 'nothingness', or the idea that the extreme subtlety of this mode of existence is akin to non-existence. Finally, abandoning even the thought of 'nothingness', there arises the ineffable state of mind known as 'neither perception nor non-perception' (level 31). This is the highest state in which anyone can be reborn. If the names of the two highest states sound familiar it is because they bear the same names as the stages of meditation attained by the Buddha under his two teachers. The Buddha gained access to these states by tuning into their 'frequency' through meditation. As we shall see, Buddhist ideas about cosmology dovetail with its meditational theory.

Karma

In the cosmology set out above, karma functions as the elevator that takes people from one floor of the building to another. Good deeds result in an upward movement and bad deeds in a downward one. Karma is not a system of rewards and punishments meted out by God but a kind of natural law akin to the law of gravity. Individuals are thus the sole authors of their good and bad fortune. In popular usage karma is thought of simply as the good and bad things that happen to people, a little like good and bad luck. The literal meaning of the Sanskrit word karma is 'action', but karma as a religious concept is concerned not with just any actions but with actions of a particular kind. Karmic actions are *moral* actions, and the Buddha defined karma by reference to moral choices and the acts consequent upon them. He stated 'It is choice (*cetanā*), O monks, that I call karma; having chosen one acts through body, speech, or mind' (A.iii.415). Moral actions are unlike other actions in that they have both transitive and intransitive effects. The transitive effect is seen in the direct impact moral actions have on others; for example, when we kill or steal, someone is deprived of his life or property. The intransitive effect is seen in the way moral actions affect the agent. According to Buddhism, human beings have free will, and in the exercise of free will they engage in self-determination. In a very real sense individuals create themselves through their moral choices. By freely and repeatedly choosing certain sorts of things, an individual shapes his character, and through his character his future. As the proverb has it: 'Sow an act, reap a habit; sow a habit, reap a character; sow a character, reap a destiny.'

Buddhism explains this process in terms of *saṅkhāras* (Sanskrit: *saṃskāras*), a difficult term usually translated as 'mental formations'. *Saṅkhāras* are the character-traits and dispositions that are formed when moral choices (*cetanā*) are made and given effect in action. The process may be likened to the work of a potter who moulds the clay into a finished shape: the soft clay is one's character, and when we make moral choices we hold ourselves in our hands and shape our natures for good or ill. It is not hard to see how even within the course of a single lifetime particular patterns of behaviour lead inexorably to certain results. Great works of literature reveal how the fate that befalls the protagonists is due not to chance but to a character flaw that leads to a tragic series of events. The remote effects of karmic choices are referred to as the 'maturation' (*vipāka*) or 'fruit' (*phala*) of the karmic act. The metaphor is an agricultural one: performing good and bad deeds is like planting seeds that will fruit at a later date. Othello's jealousy, Macbeth's ruthless ambition, and Hamlet's hesitation and self-doubt would all be seen by Buddhists as *saṅkhāras*; the tragic outcome in each case would be the inevitable 'fruit' (*phala*) of the choices these character-traits predisposed the individual to make.

Not all the consequences of what a person does are experienced in the lifetime in which the deeds are performed. Karma that has been accumulated but not yet experienced is carried forward to the next life, or even many lifetimes ahead. Buddhists disagree on exactly how this happens, but one possibility is that the performance of good deeds is like charging up a battery with karmic energy, which is then stored until a future time. Certain key aspects of a person's next rebirth are thought of as karmically determined. These include the family into which one is born, one's social status, physical appearance, and of course, one's character and personality, since these are simply carried over from the previous life. Some Buddhists adopt a fatalistic perspective and see every piece of good and bad luck as due to some karmic cause. The doctrine of karma, however, does not claim that everything that happens to a person is karmically determined. Many of the things that happen in life—like winning the lottery or breaking a leg—may simply be accidents. Karma does not determine precisely what will happen or how anyone will react to what happens. Individuals are free to resist previous conditioning and establish new patterns of behaviour: such, indeed, is the point of becoming a Buddhist.

What, then, makes an action good or bad? From the Buddha's definition above it can be seen to be largely a matter of intention and choice. The psychological springs of motivation are described in Buddhism as 'roots', and there are said to be three good roots and three bad roots. Actions motivated by greed, hatred, and delusion are bad (*akusala*, Sanskrit: *akuśala*) while actions motivated by their opposites—non-attachment, benevolence, and understanding—are good (*kusala*, Sanskrit: *kuśala*). Making progress to enlightenment, however, is not simply a matter of having good intentions, and evil is sometimes done by people who act from the highest motives. Good intentions, therefore, must find expression in right actions, and right actions are basically those which do no harm to either oneself or others. The kinds of actions which fail these requirements are prohibited in various sets of precepts, about which more will be said when discussing ethics.

Merit

Karma can be either good or bad. Buddhists speak of good karma as 'merit' (*puñña*, Sanskrit: *puṇya*), and much effort is expended in acquiring it. Some picture it as a kind of spiritual capital—like money in a bank account—whereby credit is built up as the deposit on a heavenly rebirth. One of the best ways for a layman to earn merit is by supporting the Order of monks. This can be done by placing food in the bowls of monks as they pass on their daily alms round, by providing robes for the monks, by listening to sermons and attending religious services, and by donating funds for the upkeep of monasteries and temples. Merit can even be made by congratulating other donors and rejoicing in their generosity. Some Buddhists make the accumulation of merit an end in itself, and go to the extreme of carrying a notebook to keep a tally of their karmic 'balance'. This is to lose sight of the fact that merit is earned as a by-product of doing what is right. To do good deeds simply to obtain good karma would be to act from a selfish motive, and would not earn much merit.

In many Buddhist cultures there is a belief in 'merit transference', or the idea that good karma can be shared with others, just like money. Donating good karma has the happy result that instead of one's own karmic balance being depleted, as it would in the case of money, it increases as a result of the generous motivation in sharing. The more one gives the more one receives! It is doubtful to what extent there is canonical authority for notions of this kind, although the motivation to share one's merit in a spirit of generosity is certainly karmically wholesome since it would lead to the formation of a generous and benevolent character.

A Western Perspective

Westerners often find the ideas of karma and rebirth puzzling. To a certain extent this is due to different cultural presuppositions about time and history, as alluded to earlier. In a culture which conceptualizes time as cyclic the idea of rebirth seems natural. But if people are reborn, it might be objected, why do so few remember previous lives? In part the explanation may be that cultural categories condition individual experience. In the absence of a framework of belief in reincarnation, memories of previous lives may go unrecognized or unacknowledged. Individuals may be unwilling to risk ridicule by reporting them. When such memories are reported by children they are commonly dismissed by teachers and parents as the product of an overactive imagination. There is, however, a growing body of testimony from individuals who claim to recall previous lives, many of which it is difficult to account for unless the memories are genuine. Nevertheless, such recollections are rare, even in cultures where rebirth is accepted. One possible explanation a Buddhist might advance for this is that the experience of death and rebirth tends to erase such recollections from the upper levels of the mind, and that these memories can only be recovered in altered states of consciousness such as the kind induced by meditation or hypnosis.

Another common question about rebirth is: 'If people are reborn, why does the population not increase more rapidly?' Again this question arises from anthropocentric assumptions. The human world is only one of the realms of rebirth, and since beings can be reborn in one of any of the six realms there is continuous movement from one to another. Some

Buddhist schools, notably those in Tibet, believe there is an intermediate state which acts as a buffer between lives and in which the spirit of the deceased person remains for up to forty-nine days before being reborn. During this time the spirit glimpses all six realms of rebirth before being attracted—as if by magnetism—to the one most in keeping with its karmic state. According to other schools, however, the transition from one life to the next is instantaneous, and death is followed immediately by conception in a new life.

Is it necessary to believe in the existence of the six realms and the heavens and hells to be a Buddhist? Not necessarily. Although most Buddhists do accept the traditional teachings, it is possible to reinterpret these in various ways as, perhaps, referring to other dimensions of existence, parallel universes, or simply states of mind. Advocates of 'Buddhist modernism', about which I will say more in the final chapter, tend to reject the more 'medieval' elements of the traditional scheme and replace them with notions more congenial to the modern age. It may even be possible to be a Buddhist and reject the idea of rebirth altogether, although this would be at the price of reducing Buddhism to something like scientific humanism. Belief in a continued personal existence in some form or other after death would seem to be a minimal requirement for most traditions of Buddhist thought.

So is the goal of Buddhism to be reborn in a more fortunate condition? Although in practice many Buddhists—both monks and laymen—fervently desire this, it is not the final solution to suffering that Buddhism seeks. The Buddha was dissatisfied with the temporary bliss he attained through the trances taught to him by his teachers, and the sublime existence enjoyed by the gods is but a prolongation of this experience. Sooner or later the good karma that results in a heavenly birth will run its course and even the gods will die and be reborn. Karmic energy is finite and eventually expires, not unlike that of a spacecraft in a decaying orbit. The answer to the problem of suffering does not lie in a better rebirth in the cycle of reincarnation (*saṃsāra*)—only nirvana offers a final solution.

4 The Four Noble Truths

*T*he ultimate goal of Buddhism is to put an end to suffering and rebirth. The Buddha stated, 'Both in the past and now, I set forth only this: suffering and the end of suffering.' Although this formulation is negative, the goal also has a positive side, because the way one puts an end to suffering is by fulfilling the human potential for goodness and happiness. Someone who achieves this complete state of self-realization is said to have attained nirvana. Nirvana is the *summum bonum* of Buddhism—the final and highest good. It is both a concept and an experience. As a concept it offers a particular vision of human fulfilment and gives contour and shape to the ideal life. As an experience it becomes incarnate over the course of time in the person who seeks it.

It should be clear why nirvana is desired, but how is it to be attained? The discussion in the preceding chapters suggests part of the answer. We know that Buddhism places a high value on a virtuous life; living morally, therefore, would appear to be a prerequisite. Some scholars, however, reject this idea. They argue that accumulating merit through the performance of good deeds actually stands in the way of nirvana. Good deeds, they point out, produce karma, and karma binds one to the cycle of rebirth. Since this is so, they reason, it follows that karma—and all other ethical considerations—must be transcended before nirvana can be attained. There are two problems with this view. The first is to explain why—if moral action is a hindrance to nirvana—the texts continually enjoin the performance of good deeds. The second difficulty is to explain why those who gain enlightenment, such as the Buddha, continue to live exemplary moral lives.

A solution to these problems may lie in the suggestion that leading a moral life is only *part* of the ideal of human perfection which nirvana represents. Thus while virtue (*sīla*, Sanskrit: *śīla*) is an essential component in this ideal it is incomplete on its own, and needs to be supplemented by something else. The other component which is required is wisdom (*paññā*, Sanskrit: *prajñā*). 'Wisdom' in Buddhism means a profound philosophical understanding of the human condition. It requires insight into the nature of reality of the kind which comes through long reflection and deep thought. It is a kind of *gnosis*, or direct apprehension of truth, which deepens over time and eventually reaches full maturity in the complete awakening experienced by the Buddha.

Nirvana, then, is a fusion of virtue and wisdom. The relationship between them might be expressed in philosophical language by saying that virtue and wisdom are both 'necessary' conditions for nirvana but neither is 'sufficient': only when the two are present together are the necessary and sufficient conditions for nirvana found. An early text likens them to two hands which wash and purify each other, and makes quite clear that a person who lacks one or the other is incomplete and unfulfilled (D.i.124).

Granted that wisdom is the essential counterpart of virtue, what is it that one must know to become enlightened? The truth that must be known is essentially that perceived by the Buddha on the night of his enlightenment and subsequently set forth in his first sermon delivered in the deer park near Benares. This sermon makes reference to four interlinked propositions known as the Four Noble Truths. These assert that (1) life is suffering, (2) suffering is caused by craving, (3) suffering can have an end, and (4) there is a path which leads to the end of suffering. Sometimes a medical metaphor is used to illustrate the relationship between them, and the Buddha is likened to a physician who has found a cure for life's ills. First he diagnoses the disease, second explains its cause, third determines that a cure exists, and fourth sets out the treatment.

The American psychiatrist M. Scott Peck begins his best-selling book *The Road Less Travelled* with the statement 'Life is difficult'. Making reference to the First Noble Truth he adds, 'This is a great truth, one of the greatest truths.' This truth, known in Buddhism as the 'Truth of Suffering', is the cornerstone of the Buddha's teaching. The Truth of Suffering states that suffering (*dukkha*, Sanskrit: *duḥkha*) is an intrinsic part of life, and it diagnoses the human condition as fundamentally one of 'dis-ease'. It makes reference to suffering of many kinds, beginning with physical or biological experiences such as birth, sickness, old age, and death. While these often involve physical pain, the deeper problem

---

1. The Truth of Suffering (Dukkha)

What, O Monks, is the Noble Truth of Suffering? Birth is suffering, sickness is suffering, old age is suffering, death is suffering. Pain, grief, sorrow, lamentation, and despair are suffering. Association with what is unpleasant is suffering, disassociation from what is pleasant is suffering. Not to get what one wants is suffering. In short, the five factors of individuality are suffering.

is the inevitability of *repeated* birth, sickness, ageing, and death in lifetime after lifetime, both for oneself and loved ones. Individuals are powerless in the face of these realities, and despite advances in medical science remain vulnerable to sickness and accident by virtue of their physical natures. In addition to physical pain, the Truth of Suffering makes reference to emotional and psychological forms of distress such as 'grief, sorrow, lamentation, and despair'. These can sometimes present more intractable problems than physical suffering: few lives are free of grief and sorrow, and there are many debilitating psychological conditions, such as chronic depression, from which a complete recovery may never be made.

Beyond these obvious examples of suffering the Truth of Suffering refers to a more subtle kind of suffering which might be termed 'existential'. This is seen in the statement 'Not to get what one wants is suffering.' The kind of suffering envisaged here is the frustration, disappointment, and disillusionment experienced when life fails to live up to our expectations and things do not go as we wish. The Buddha was no morbid pessimist and certainly knew from his own experience as a young prince that life can have its pleasant moments. The problem, however, is that the good times do not last; sooner or later they fade away, or one becomes bored with what once seemed novel and full of promise. In this context the word *dukkha* has a more abstract and pervasive sense: it suggests that even when life is not painful it can be unsatisfactory and unfulfilling. In this and many other contexts 'unsatisfactoriness' captures the meaning of *dukkha* better than 'suffering'.

Towards the end of the formulation, the Truth of Suffering suggests a fundamental reason why human life can never be ultimately satisfying. The statement 'the five factors of individuality are suffering' is a reference to a teaching expounded by the Buddha in his second sermon (*Vin*.i.13) which analyses human nature into five factors, namely the physical body (*rūpa*), sensations and feelings (*vedanā*), cognitions (*saññā*), character traits and dispositions (*sankhāra*), and consciousness or sentiency (*viññāna*). There is no need to go into detail about the five factors individually since the important point for us here is not so much what the list includes as what it does not. Specifically, the doctrine makes no mention of a soul or Self, understood as an eternal and immutable spiritual essence. By adopting this position the Buddha set himself apart from the orthodox Indian religious tradition known as Brahmanism, which claimed that each person possesses an eternal soul (*ātman*) which is either part of, or identical with, a metaphysical absolute known as Brahman (a sort of impersonal godhead).

The Buddha said he could find no evidence for the existence of either the personal soul (*ātman*) or its cosmic counterpart (*brahman*). Instead his approach was practical and empirical, more akin to psychology than theology. He explained human nature as constituted by the five factors much in the way that an automobile is constituted by its wheels, transmission, engine, steering, and chassis. Unlike science, of course, he believed that a person's moral identity—what we might call the individual's 'spiritual DNA'—survives death and is reborn. In stating that the five factors of individuality are *suffering*, however, the Buddha was pointing out that human nature cannot provide a foundation for permanent happiness because the doctrine of the five factors shows that the individual has no real core. Because human beings are made up of these five constantly shifting components it is inevitable that sooner or later suffering will arise, just as an automobile will eventually wear out and break down. Suffering is thus engrained in the very fabric of our being.

The content of the Truth of Suffering is supplied in part from the Buddha's vision of the first three of the four signs—

the old man, the sick man, and the corpse—and his realization that life is shot through with suffering and unhappiness of all kinds. Many who encounter Buddhism find this assessment of the human condition pessimistic. To this, Buddhists tend to reply that their religion is neither pessimistic nor optimistic, but realistic, and that the Truth of Suffering simply presents the facts of life in an objective way. If the presentation seems pessimistic it is due to the inveterate human tendency to shrink from unpleasant truths and 'look on the bright side'. No doubt this was the reason why the Buddha observed that the Truth of Suffering was extremely hard to grasp. It is akin to admitting that one has a serious disease, something no one wishes to acknowledge, yet until the condition is recognized there can be no hope of a cure.

Granted that life is suffering, how does this suffering arise? The second noble truth—the Truth of Arising (*samudāya*)—explains that suffering arises from craving or 'thirst' (*taṇhā*, Sanskrit: *tṛṣṇā*). Craving fuels suffering in the way that wood fuels a fire: in a vivid metaphor in the Fire Sermon (S.iv.19) the Buddha spoke of all human experience as being 'ablaze' with desire. Fire is an appropriate metaphor for desire since it consumes what it feeds on without being satisfied. It spreads rapidly, becomes attached to new objects, and burns with the pain of unassuaged longing.

2. The Truth of Arising (Samudāya)

This, O Monks, is the Truth of the Arising of Suffering. It is this thirst or craving (*taṇhā*) which gives rise to rebirth, which is bound up with passionate delight and which seeks fresh pleasure now here and now there in the form of (1) thirst for sensual pleasure, (2) thirst for existence, and (3) thirst for non-existence.

It is desire, in the form of a strong addiction to life and the pleasant experiences it offers, that causes rebirth. If the five factors of individuality are likened to a car, then desire is the fuel that propels it forward. Although rebirth is normally thought of as taking place from life to life, it also happens from moment to moment: a person is said to be reborn from second to second as the five factors of individuality change and interact, driven by the thirst for pleasurable experiences. The continuity of individual existence from one life to the next is simply the result of the accumulated momentum of desire.

The Truth of Arising states that craving or thirst manifests itself in three main forms, the first of which is thirst for sensual pleasure. This takes the form of craving for gratification through the objects of the senses, such as the desire to experience pleasant tastes, sensations, odours, sights, and sounds. The second is thirst for existence. This refers to the deep instinctual will to *be* which drives us on to new lives and new experiences. The third way that craving manifests itself is as the desire not to possess, but to destroy. This is the shadow side of desire, manifested in the impulse to negate, deny, and reject that which is unpleasant or unwelcome. The desire to destroy can also lead to self-denying and self-negating behaviour. Low self-esteem and thoughts such as 'I'm no good', or 'I'm a failure', are manifestations of this attitude when directed towards the self. In extreme forms it can lead to physically self-destructive behaviour such as suicide. The kind of physical austerities the Buddha eventually rejected can also be seen as an expression of this impulse towards self-negation.

So does this mean that all desire is wrong? We must be careful before drawing this conclusion. Although 'desire' is often used as a translation for *taṇhā*, the English word has a much broader semantic range. *Taṇhā* is more restricted in meaning, and connotes desire that has become perverted in some sense, usually by being excessive or wrongly directed. Its aim is usually sensory stimulation and pleasure. Not all desires, however, are of this kind, and Buddhist sources often speak of desire in a more positive light using the term *chanda*. Having positive goals for oneself and others (such as attaining nirvana), desiring that others should be happy, and wishing to leave the world a better place than one found it, are all examples of positive and wholesome desires which do not count as *taṇhā*.

Whereas wrong desires restrict and fetter, right desires enhance and liberate. We might use smoking as an example to illustrate the difference. The desire of a chain-smoker for another cigarette is *taṇhā*, since its aim is nothing more than short-term gratification. Such a desire is compulsive, limiting and cyclic: it leads nowhere but to the next cigarette (and, as a side effect, to ill health). The desire of a chain-smoker to give up smoking, on the other hand, would be a virtuous desire since it would break the cyclic pattern of a compulsive negative habit and enhance health and well-being.

In the Truth of Arising *taṇhā* stands for the 'three roots of evil' mentioned above, namely greed, hatred, and delusion. In Buddhist art these are pictured as a cock, a pig, and a snake chasing around in a small circle at the centre of the 'Wheel of Life' depicted in Chapter Three, with their tails in each others' mouths. Since craving only gives rise to further craving, the cycle of rebirth goes round and round, and individuals are born again and again. How this comes about is explained in detail in a teaching known as 'origination-in-dependence' (*paṭicca-samuppāda*, Sanskrit: *pratītya-samutpāda*). This doctrine explains how craving and ignorance lead to rebirth in a sequence of twelve stages. Rather than discuss the twelve stages it is more important for our present purposes to grasp the underlying principle, which applies not just to human psychology but to reality at large.

At its most basic level the doctrine could be summed up as

the claim that every effect has a cause: in other words, every-thing which comes into being originates in dependence on something else (or on a number of other things). On this view, all phenomena arise as part of a causal series, and nothing exists independently in and for itself. The universe, therefore, comes to be seen not as a collection of more or less static objects but a dynamic network of interrelated causes and effects. Moreover, just as the human person can be analysed into the five factors of individuality with nothing left over, so all phenomena can be reduced to their constituent parts without finding anything 'essential' in them. Everything which comes into being is said to bear three characteristics or 'marks' namely unsatisfactoriness (*dukkha*), impermanence (*anicca*), and the absence of self-essence (*anattā*). Things are unsatisfactory because they are impermanent (hence unstable and unreliable), and they are impermanent because they lack a self-nature which is independent of the universal causal process.

It can be seen that the Buddhist universe is characterized primarily by cyclic change: at the psychological level in the endless process of craving and gratification; at the personal level in the sequence of death and rebirth; and at the cosmic level in the creation and destruction of galaxies. Underlying all of this is the principle of cause and effect set out in the doctrine of origination-in-dependence, the implications of which were developed in a profound way in later Buddhism.

The third noble truth is the Truth of Cessation (*nirodha*).

---

3. The Truth of Cessation (Nirodha)

This, O Monks, is the Truth of the Cessation of Suffering. It is the utter cessation of that craving (*taṇhā*), the withdrawal from it, the renouncing of it, the rejection of it, liberation from it, non-attachment to it.

This Truth announces that when craving is removed suffering ceases and nirvana is attained. As will be recalled from the story of the Buddha's life, nirvana takes two forms: the first occurs during life and the second at death. The Buddha attained what is known as 'nirvana-in-this-life' while sitting under a tree at the age of 35. At the age of 80 he passed away into 'final nirvana' from which he would not be reborn.

'Nirvana' literally means 'quenching' or 'blowing out', in the way that the flame of a candle is blown out. But what is it that is 'blown out'? Is it one's soul, one's ego, one's identity? It cannot be the soul that is blown out, since Buddhism denies that any such thing exists. Nor is it the ego or one's sense of identity that disappears, although nirvana certainly involves a radically transformed state of consciousness which is free of the obsession with 'me and mine'. What is extinguished, in fact, is the triple fire of greed, hatred, and delusion which leads to rebirth. Indeed, the simplest definition of nirvana-in-this-life is as 'the end of greed, hatred, and delusion' (S.38.1). It is clear that nirvana-in-this-life is a psychological and ethical reality, a transformed state of personality characterized by peace, deep spiritual joy, compassion, and a refined and subtle awareness. Negative mental states and emotions such as doubt, worry, anxiety, and fear are absent from the enlightened mind. Saints in many religious traditions exhibit some or all of these qualities, and ordinary people also possess them to some degree, although imperfectly developed. An enlightened person, however, such as a Buddha or an Arhat, possesses them all completely.

What becomes of such a person at death? It is in connection with final nirvana that problems of understanding arise. When the flame of craving is extinguished, rebirth ceases, and an enlightened person is not reborn. So what has happened to him? There is no clear answer to this question in the early sources. The Buddha said that asking about the whereabouts of 'an enlightened one' after death is like asking where a flame goes when it is blown out. The flame, of course, has not 'gone' anywhere: it is simply the process of combustion that has ceased. Removing craving and ignorance is like taking away the oxygen and fuel which a flame needs to burn. The image of the blowing out of the flame, however, should not be taken as suggesting that final nirvana is annihilation: the sources make quite clear that this would be a mistake, as would the conclusion that nirvana is the eternal existence of a personal soul.

The Buddha discouraged speculation about the nature of nirvana and emphasized instead the need to strive for its attainment. Those who asked speculative questions about nirvana he compared to a man wounded by a poisoned arrow who, rather than pulling the arrow out, persists in asking for irrelevant information about the man who fired it, such as his name and clan, how far away he was standing, and so forth (M.i.426). In keeping with this reluctance on the part of the Buddha to elaborate on the question, the early sources describe nirvana in predominantly negative terms such as 'the absence of desire', 'the extinction of thirst', 'blowing out', and 'cessation'. A smaller number of positive epithets are also found including 'the auspicious', 'the good', 'purity', 'peace', 'truth', and 'the further shore'. Certain passages seem to suggest that nirvana is a transcendent reality which is 'unborn, unoriginated, uncreated and unformed' (*Udāna* 80), but it is difficult to know what interpretation to place upon such formulations. In the last analysis the nature of final nirvana remains an enigma other than to those who experience it. What we *can* be sure of, however, is that it means the end of suffering and rebirth.

The Fourth Noble Truth, that of the Path or Way (*magga*, Sanskrit: *mārga*), explains how the transition from *saṃsāra* to nirvana is to be made. In the hustle and bustle of everyday life few stop to ponder the most fulfilling way to live. Questions of this kind exercised the Greek philosophers, and

4. The Truth of the Path (Magga)

This, O Monks, is the Truth of the Path which leads to the cessation of suffering. It is this Noble Eightfold Path, which consists of (1) Right View, (2) Right Resolve, (3) Right Speech, (4) Right Action, (5) Right Livelihood, (6) Right Effort, (7) Right Mindfulness, (8) Right Meditation.

the Buddha had his own contribution to make. He thought that the highest form of life was one which led to the development of virtue and knowledge, and the Eightfold Path sets forth a way of life designed to bring these to fruition.

The Eightfold Path is known as the 'Middle Way' because it steers a course between a life of indulgence and one of harsh austerity. It consists of eight factors divided into the three categories of Morality, Meditation, and Wisdom. These define the parameters of human good and indicate where the scope for human flourishing lies. In the division known as Morality (*sīla*), the moral virtues are perfected, and in the division known as Wisdom (*paññā*), the intellectual virtues are developed. What about Meditation? The role of meditation will be examined in more detail in the following chapter, so I will not say much about it at this point except to note that it supports the other two.

Although the Path consists of eight factors, they should not be thought of as stages which are passed through on the way to nirvana then left behind. Instead, the eight factors exemplify the ways in which Morality, Meditation, and Wisdom are to be cultivated on a continuing basis. *Right View* means first, the acceptance of Buddhist teachings and later their experiential confirmation. *Right Resolve* means making a serious commitment to developing right attitudes. *Right Speech* means telling the truth and speaking in a thoughtful and sensitive way. *Right Action* means abstaining from wrongful bodily behaviour such as killing, stealing, or behaving wrongfully with respect to sensual pleasures. *Right Livelihood* means not engaging in an occupation which causes harm to others. *Right Effort* means gaining control of one's thoughts and cultivating positive states of mind. *Right Mindfulness* means cultivating constant awareness, and *Right Meditation* means developing deep levels of mental calm through various techniques which concentrate the mind and integrate the personality.

1. Right Understanding
2. Right Resolve } Wisdom *(Paññā)*

3. Right Speech
4. Right Action } Morality *(Sīla)*
5. Right Livelihood

6. Right Effort
7. Right Mindfulness } Meditation *(Samādhi)*
8. Right Meditation

The Eightfold Path and its Three Divisions

In this respect the practice of the Eightfold Path is a kind of modelling process: the eight factors reveal how a Buddha would live, and by living like a Buddha one gradually becomes one. The Eightfold Path is thus a path of self-transformation: an intellectual, emotional, and moral restructuring in which a person is reoriented from selfish, limited objectives towards a horizon of possibilities and opportunities for fulfilment. Through the pursuit of knowledge *(paññā)* and moral virtue *(sīla)*, ignorance and selfish desire are overcome, the cause of the arising of suffering is removed, and nirvana is attained.

5 The Mahāyāna

*T*he Buddha appointed no successor and left his followers to interpret the Dharma for themselves. It was not long before disagreements arose, initially on matters of monastic practice and later on doctrine, and in the absence of any central authority, the development of variant traditions was almost inevitable. The most serious disagreement occurred around a century after the Buddha's death between a group later designated the 'Elders' (*Sthaviras*), and another known as the 'Universal Assembly' (*Mahāsaṅghikas*).

The Great Schism

What did the two disagree over? The records give conflicting accounts. Some attribute the schism to a doctrinal dispute which turned on the status of the Buddha as compared with an Arhat. According to this version of events, a monk named Mahādeva advanced 'Five Theses' suggesting that an Arhat was inferior to a Buddha in certain respects, such as not having completely extirpated craving, and in lacking the omniscience which it was now claimed the Buddha possessed (the Buddha had not claimed this himself). The most likely cause of the schism, however, appears to have been an attempt by the Elders to modify the Monastic Rule by introducing additional rules of conduct.

Underlying the schism were the more general stresses and strains which occurred as Buddhism began to spread beyond its home territory to other parts of India. As it expanded it encountered new customs and new ideas. How should it respond? Should it hold fast to the old ways, or change to accommodate new beliefs and practices? In the end opinion polarized on a range of issues and the two groups went their separate ways in what became known as the 'Great Schism'. In due course both the Elders and the Universal Assembly fragmented into a number of sub-schools. All of these have now since died out, with the exception of the Theravāda, which is descended from the Elder tradition. However, many of these early schools left a legacy in the contribution they made to a revolutionary new movement which became known as the Mahāyāna.

The Mahāyāna

Mahāyāna means the 'Great Vehicle', and is so called because it regards itself as the universal way to salvation. The early formative period of the movement occurs around the time of Christ, and may be dated roughly between 100 BC and AD 100. Although there is no firm evidence of influence either way between Christianity and Buddhism, there are some similarities between Christianity and Mahāyāna Buddhism which it might be helpful to note. The first concerns the concept of a saviour. Just as Christianity holds up Christ's self-sacrifice as a model for Christian service to others, so the highest ideal in the Mahāyāna is a life dedicated to the well-being of the world. Rather than seeking one's own salvation, in the way the earlier teachings had advised, the Mahāyāna places great emphasis on working to save others. This finds expression in the ideal of the bodhisattva, someone who takes a vow to work tirelessly over countless life-times to lead others to nirvana. Everyone who subscribes to the Mahāyāna technically becomes a bodhisattva, but for most this is just the starting point of their long course of spiritual development. So important was the bodhisattva ideal that, particularly in its early stages, the Mahāyāna was known simply as the *Bodhisattva-yāna*, or the 'Vehicle of the Bodhisattvas'.

Linked to the idea of service to others is the notion of self-less love. Jesus gave love (*agapē*) great prominence in his teachings, and in the Mahāyāna compassion (*karuṇā*) is accorded a central place. Indeed, it is compassion for the suffering of others which motivates a bodhisattva to sacrifice himself on their behalf. Of course, a bodhisattva cannot 'redeem' others as Christ did. Instead, he devotes his efforts to becoming a 'good friend' to beings. He helps them by example, by reducing their sufferings in practical ways, by encouraging and helping them, and by teaching them the path to liberation.

The Buddha

As the figure of the bodhisattva comes more into the fore-ground, that of the Buddha begins to recede and become more sublime. By the time the Mahāyāna came into being, the Buddha had been dead for several centuries, and as the accounts of his life became more exaggerated and embel-lished, he came to be thought of as a semi-divine being. This mystique was heightened by the ambiguity surrounding his status in final nirvana. although the Elders taught that he had passed beyond this world into final nirvana, it was also possible to conceive of him as existing in a transcendent realm. Followers of the Mahāyāna reasoned that a being as compassionate as the Buddha would never cut himself off from others: they believed he was still 'out there' somewhere, actively working for the welfare of beings just as he had on earth. In line with this belief, devotional cults sprang up in which reverence and homage were offered and intercessions sought. If a bodhisattva resembles Christ in the love and service he gave to mankind, then the Buddha came to resemble God the Father as a benevolent supernatural being, not located in the world but positioned somewhere close by in a heavenly realm and taking a keen fatherly interest in the welfare of his children.

Eventually these ideas gave birth to a full-blown Mahāyāna cosmology and new 'Buddhology', which envisaged the Buddha as having 'three bodies' (*trikāya*) or existing in three dimensions: earthly, heavenly, and transcendent. The earthly body (*nirmāṇakāya*) was the human body he had on earth. His heavenly body (*sambhogakāya*) was in a blissful realm located somewhere 'upstream' from the world we now inhabit, not unlike the Christian heaven. The transcendent body (*dharmakāya*) was the Buddha conceived of as identical with ultimate truth, in some respects not unlike the way Christian mystics and philosophers have spoken of God as the Absolute or ultimate reality (Mahāyāna schools understand these terms in various ways). One final resemblance to Christian doctrine might be mentioned: just as there will be a 'Second Coming' on the Day of Judgement, the belief arose that a Buddha known as Maitreya would appear at the end of the present eon when there would be a utopian era in which multitudes would gain enlightenment. This idea (which is also found in Theravāda Buddhism) laid the basis for a number of Messianic cults which have been popular from time to time throughout both north and south Asia.

The significance of the division that occurred in Buddhism with the rise of the Mahāyāna is not unlike that which took place at the Reformation when Latin Christianity fissured into the Catholic and Protestant churches. Both divisions left

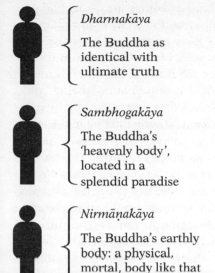

Dharmakāya

The Buddha as identical with ultimate truth

Sambhogakāya

The Buddha's 'heavenly body', located in a splendid paradise

Nirmāṇakāya

The Buddha's earthly body: a physical, mortal, body like that of any human being

The Buddha's 'Three Bodies' (trikāya)

an enduring mark on the religious landscape, and Buddhists think of themselves either as Mahāyānists or Theravādins just as Christians would identify themselves as either Catholic or Protestant. There are also doctrinal similarities in that both Protestantism and early Buddhism see salvation as primarily an individual responsibility, while Catholicism (as also the Orthodox churches) and Mahāyāna Buddhism accept that help and intercession are possible through the agency of saints and bodhisattvas. It would be unwise to press these comparisons too far, since there are also many differences. The Mahāyāna, for example, initially had the character of a loose movement and was not organized along sectarian lines. Nor was there a radical separation between followers of the Mahāyāna and other schools, and it was not uncommon for monks ordained in the Universal Assembly, or even branches of the Elder tradition, to have Mahāyāna sympathies while living in communion with brethren who did not.

Mahāyāna Sūtras

The nucleus of the Mahāyāna was a series of new scriptures which appeared in the early centuries of the Christian era. Whereas the earlier *sūtras* contained in the Pali Canon were believed to be the Buddha's own words, the new *sūtras* could not easily be attributed to the founder. These texts—which were all composed anonymously and often show the work of many hands—none the less came to have great authority because they seemed visionary and inspired. The new Mahāyāna cosmology, furthermore, made it possible to claim that the Buddha was, if not the human author of the new *sūtras*, at least the spiritual one, since his wisdom continued to emanate from the higher levels of the cosmos down to the human sphere.

The major Mahāyāna *sūtras*, such as the *Lotus Sūtra* (AD *c*200) embark on a drastic revisioning of early Buddhist history. They claim, in essence, that although the historical Buddha had appeared to live and die like an ordinary man, he had, in reality, been enlightened from time immemorial. As a wise and compassionate teacher, however, he had gone through an elaborate charade to accommodate the expectations of the people of the time. Just as an experienced teacher would not teach an advanced topic such as calculus to students just beginning mathematics, so the Buddha had revealed only limited teachings—a spiritual *ABC*—which he knew his early followers could assimilate. The reason for this was that the true depth and scope of the Dharma—now fully revealed in the Mahāyāna—was profound beyond measure, and rather than confuse and overwhelm people the Buddha

सद्धर्मपुण्डरीकसूत्रम् ।

॥ नमः सर्वबुद्धबोधिसत्त्वेभ्यः । नमः सर्वतथागतप्रत्येकबुद्धार्यश्रावकेभ्यो-
ऽतीतानागतप्रत्युत्पन्नेभ्यश्च बोधिसत्त्वेभ्यः ॥

१ निदानपरिवर्तः ।

एवं मया श्रुतम् । एकस्मिन् समये भगवान् राजगृहे विहरति स्म गृध्रकूटे पर्वते ५
महता भिक्षुसंघेन सार्धं द्वादशभिर्भिक्षुशतैः सर्वैरर्हद्भिः क्षीणास्त्रवैर्निःक्लेशैर्वशीभूतैः सुवि-
मुक्तचित्तैः सुविमुक्तप्रज्ञैर्राजानेयैर्महानागैः कृतकृत्यैः कृतकरणीयैरपहृतभारैरनुप्राप्तस्वकार्थैः
परिक्षीणभवसंयोजनैः सम्यगाज्ञासुविमुक्तचित्तैः सर्वचेतोवशितापरमपारमिताप्राप्तैरभिज्ञाता-
भिज्ञातैर्महाश्रावकैः । तद्यथा-आयुष्मता च आज्ञातकौण्डिन्येन, आयुष्मता च अश्वजिता,
आयुष्मता च बाष्पेण, आयुष्मता च महानाम्ना, आयुष्मता च भद्रिकेण, आयुष्मता च १०
महाकाश्यपेन, आयुष्मता च उरुबिल्वकाश्यपेन, आयुष्मता च नदीकाश्यपेन, आयुष्मता

5. *Sanskrit Text of the Lotus Sūtra*

had used 'skilful means' (*upāya-kauśalya*) to put the truth
before them in a simplified form.

There is a famous passage in the *Lotus Sūtra*—the Parable
of the Burning House—which compares the Buddha to a
wise parent who, seeing that the house his children are in is
ablaze, ponders how best to lead them to safety. The children, being engrossed in their games, do not realize the danger they are in and are reluctant to leave. The Buddha,
therefore, promises the children that new toys await them
outside, and the excited children follow him out and are
saved from the flames. In the parable, the burning house
stands for *saṃsāra*—the world of suffering and impermanence—and the children are the early followers. Since they are
childish and self-absorbed, the Buddha appeals to them by
promising teachings of the kind he knows they will find
attractive. Now that the children have been saved from the
immediate danger, however, the full truth can be revealed.

The Mahāyāna perspective, then, is that the early doctrines—although not false—were incomplete, and a 'second turning of the wheel of the Dharma' was required for them to be fulfilled. The Mahāyāna *sūtras* often poke fun at the earlier schools—which it dubbed derogatively the Hīnayāna or 'Inferior vehicle'. Some, like the highly popular *Teachings of Vimalakīrti* (AD *c*400), portray the learned monks of the early tradition being baffled by, a mere layman, Vimalakīrti, as he playfully reveals the higher teachings of the Mahāyāna.

What followers of the Mahāyāna sought above all through their religious practice was to follow the bodhisattva path. Over the course of several centuries the various stages in the 'career' of a bodhisattva were worked out in some detail. The crucial initial stage is the arising of what is known as the 'thought of enlightenment' or *bodhicitta*. This might be likened to a conversion experience, and is the point at which the initial motivation to become a bodhisattva in order to save others arises. The individual then seeks initiation as a bodhisattva, in the course of which he takes a vow (*praṇidhāna*) to save all beings by leading them to nirvana, regardless of how long it takes.

Central to a bodhisattva's practice are six virtues known as the Six Perfections (see text box). As the bodhisattva practises these perfections he progresses through a scheme of ten

---

Mahāyāna Virtues

The Six Perfections *(pāramitās)* of a Bodhisattva are:

1. Generosity (*dāna*)
2. Morality (*śīla*)
3. Patience (*kṣānti*)
4. Courage (*vīrya*)
5. Meditation (*samādhi*)
6. Wisdom (*prajñā*)

stages (*bhūmi*) each of which is a major landmark on the way to nirvana. Once he reaches the seventh stage it is impossible for him to fall back, and it is certain that he will reach nirvana. Although this scheme constitutes a reformulation of the early teachings, the new way to nirvana is not radically different to that taught in the Eightfold Path, and it can be seen that the three divisions of the latter—Morality, Meditation, and Wisdom—feature among the Six Perfections.

Bodhisattvas who had reached the higher stages of their careers were visualized as enormously powerful beings, virtually identical to the Buddha in his heavenly form. Indeed, the distinction between a Buddha and an advanced bodhisattva becomes extremely blurred. Two of the most important in the ranks of these 'celestial' bodhisattvas are Avalokiteśvara, 'The Lord who Looks Down (in compassion)' (see p. 68), and Mañjuśrī, 'Gentle Glory'. The former (of whom the Tibetan Dalai Lamas are said to be incarnations) epitomizes compassion (*karuṇā*) and the latter wisdom (*prajñā*). Avalokiteśvara is depicted as having many arms, outstretched to help suffering beings, while Mañjuśrī carries the flaming sword of wisdom which cuts through ignorance. Alongside these, a rich pantheon of Buddhas and bodhisattvas comes into being, conceived of as inhabiting a majestic unseen universe. Just as our own world-system was graced by a Buddha, it seemed not unreasonable to suppose that others had been too. The Mahāyāna therefore proceeded to invent names and characteristics for these fictional Buddhas and located them in magnificent Buddha-realms. A 'family' of five Buddhas became standard, often depicted in circular mystic diagrams known as *maṇḍalas*. A common arrangement in these colourful diagrams is to find the historical Buddha Śākyamuni (Pali: Sakyamuni) located at the centre of a circle with four ahistorical Buddhas located around him to the north, south, east, and west.

6. *The bodhisattva Avalokitésvara, the embodiment of compassion*: The bodhisattva's many arms symbolize his compassion. The extended arms hold a rosary and a lotus. Sometimes he is shown with a thousand arms and faces, indicating that his compassion is universal and inexhaustible. Chahar, Inner Mongolia, AD *c*.1700

The Buddha located in the western region was known as Amitābha ('Infinite Light'). In east Asian Buddhism, he became the centre of a popular cult which developed around the magnificent paradise or 'Pure Land' he was thought to inhabit. Amitābha (known in Japan as Amida) took a vow that if he gained enlightenment he would assist anyone who called upon his name in a spirit of faith by ensuring that they would be reborn in his Pure Land, known as *Sukhāvatī* ('Blessed with Happiness'). It is clear that with developments of this kind, which occurred within the early centuries AD, the Mahāyāna had moved some way from the Buddha's original teaching that salvation was an individual responsibility, and had come close to accepting that it could be attained through faith and grace. Even in the Pure Land school however—where ideas of this kind were developed—the western paradise of Amitābha was not seen as the same as nirvana, and a person reborn there would still need to make a final effort to gain enlightenment for himself.

Philosophical Developments

As the new *sūtras* multiplied, Buddhist teachers began to compose commentaries and treatises setting forth the philosophical basis of Mahāyāna beliefs. The most famous of these philosophers was Nāgārjuna, who lived around AD 150, and founded a school known as the *Madhyamaka* or 'Middle School'. He used the traditional concept of the 'middle way' in a sophisticated dialectical manner, and in so doing pushed the implications of certain of the early teachings to their logical conclusion. When discussing the Truth of Arising in Chapter Four, reference was made to the doctrine of origination-in-dependence. The early Theravāda scholastic tradition, known as the Abhidhamma ('higher dharma'), had understood this doctrine as referring to the origination and destruction of real elements, which they termed 'dharmas'.

Dharmas were thought of as the building-blocks of which all phenomena were composed. They were conceived of as impermanent, but none the less real. On this basis, objects such as tables and chairs were analysed as compounds of elements rather than as entities having an enduring nature of their own. A chair, for example, might be seen as consisting only of legs, a seat, and a back: there is no 'chair' over and above these parts.

Nāgārjuna, however, interpreted the doctrine of origination-in-dependence in a more radical way. He taught that dharmas were not just impermanent, but lacked any inherent reality at all. He summed this up by saying that all phenomena—tables, chairs, mountains, people—are simply *empty* of any real being. The Madhyamaka argued strongly, however, that this was not a doctrine of nihilism: the teaching does not claim that things do not exist, merely that they do not exist as independent realities in the way people normally assume. It claimed that the true status of phenomena is something midway between existence and non-existence, and it was from this interpretation of the 'middle way' that the school derived its name.

This line of thought had another important implication, namely that there can be no difference between nirvana and the realm of cyclic rebirth (*saṃsāra*). If everything is void of real existence, Nāgārjuna reasoned, then in a profound sense everything is on the same footing, so on what basis can the distinction between nirvana and *saṃsāra* be made? No difference can be found in things themselves since they are all ultimately 'empty;' the difference, therefore, must lie in our perception of them. The example is given of the person who mistakes a coil of rope for a snake at twilight and becomes terrified. When he realizes his mistake his fear subsides and his desire to run away disappears. What is needed for liberation, then, Nāgārjuna reasoned, is essentially correct vision—to see things as they really are—rather than to embark on a flight from one supposedly imperfect reality (*saṃsāra*) to a better one (nirvana). Nirvana is thus reinterpreted by the Madhyamaka as a purified vision of what is seen by the ignorant as *saṃsāra*. It follows that nirvana is here and now if we could but see it. The removal of spiritual ignorance (*avidyā*) and the realization that things are empty destroys the fear—or craving—we have for them. Nāgārjuna and his followers called this complex of ideas 'the doctrine of emptiness' (*śūnyavāda*) and it has been the inspiration of Mahāyāna thought down the centuries, generating countless commentaries and treatises.

In addition to the doctrine of emptiness, many further complex philosophical systems arose, such as the teaching of 'mind only' (*citta-mātra*), a form of idealism which sees consciousness as the sole reality and denies objective existence to material objects. Meditative experience seems to have played an important part in the development of this school as can be seen from its alternative name—the Yogācāra, or 'Practice of Yoga'. There is insufficient space here to do justice to the complexity of these ideas, or to the richness and variety of Mahāyāna thought in general, and the reader is referred to the sources at the end of the book for further particulars.

Summary

None of the Buddha's early teachings is rejected by the Mahāyāna, although they are sometimes reinterpreted in radical ways. The Mahāyāna saw itself as recovering their true meaning which, it claimed, had been lost sight of by the early tradition. Indeed, much of what is found in the Mahāyāna is not new. For example, the notion of selfless compassion—which finds expression in the bodhisattva ideal—was already evident in the Buddha's life of service to others. The doctrine of emptiness can be seen in embryonic form in the teachings on impermanence and no-self. Finally, the meditator's experience of the mind in the higher trances as luminous and pure, could easily foreshadow the conclusion that consciousness itself is the underlying reality.

The areas where the Mahāyāna was most innovative were in its revamped Buddhology and the devotional cults which sprang up around the various Buddhas and bodhisattvas. The north-west of India was an early nucleus of the Mahāyāna, and scholars have speculated about possible Hellenistic and Zoroastrian influence on Buddhism which may account for these developments. This region was a cultural melting pot into which many ideas flowed, along with goods and commodities from the Asian trade routes. Intriguing though these speculations are, however, there is no real need to invoke the idea of external influence to explain the upsurge of devotionalism in Buddhism. For one thing, devotional cults were also popular within India, and the worship of the Hindu god Krishna antedates Christ by several centuries. For another, it is possible to see signs of a cult of the Buddha and other charismatic saints even from the earliest times. On balance it is most likely that devotionalism—along with the other innovations mentioned in this chapter—was an autonomous development which arose naturally at a certain cycle in the evolution of Buddhism as ideas implicit in the early teachings were worked out.

6 Buddhism in Asia

Ashoka

From the outset Buddhism was a missionary religion. The Buddha travelled over a large area spreading his teachings, and explicitly charged his disciples to do likewise with the words: 'Go, monks, and wander for the good and welfare of the multitudes.' The spread of Buddhism was given a considerable boost in the third century BC when one of the greatest figures in Indian history—Ashoka Maurya—became emperor of India around 268 BC. Through conquest Ashoka extended the Mauryan empire, making it the largest Indian empire to be seen until the British Raj. After a bloody campaign on the east coast, in the region of present-day Orissa, he experienced remorse and turned to Buddhism. For the remainder of his long reign he ruled according to Buddhist principles, and under his patronage Buddhism flourished. As well as helping to establish Buddhism within India, Ashoka also dispatched ambassadors to the courts of rulers in the Near East and Macedonia, and, according to the Sinhalese chronicles, to South-East Asia. The record of these early missions is found in the stone inscriptions Ashoka left throughout his realm, which provide some of the most reliable data

on early Indian history. It is not known with any certainty
what became of the missions, but the ones to the West seem
to have had little impact, as the earliest surviving mention of
Buddhism in Western documents is found in the writings of
Clement of Alexandria in the second century AD (earlier classical references to the Indian *sarmanes* and *samanaioi* may
also refer to Buddhism).

Buddhism in India

In India itself great universities were established such as the
one at Nālandā near the site of modern-day Patna, which
flourished between the seventh and twelfth centuries. As
many as ten thousand students were enrolled there at any
time pursuing courses in the various branches of Buddhist
learning, such as logic, grammar, epistemology, medicine,
and the study of Madhyamaka and other philosophies.
Important centres of Buddhism also sprang up both in the
south and the far north-west, the latter an important gateway to central Asia and the far east.

During the first half of the first millennium AD Buddhism
prospered, although it suffered a setback around AD 450
when a tribe from central Asia known as the White Huns
destroyed Buddhist monasteries in Afghanistan and the
north-west of India. In the second half of the millennium
the fortunes of Buddhism were mixed, and by the end of the
period it was in decline in India. Late in the tenth century the
north once again came under attack. This time the invaders
were Muslim Turks who embarked on a long series of campaigns in the course of which they penetrated far to the
north-east of India bringing them into contact with the
ancient homeland of Buddhism. These campaigns took
the form of raids motivated by the desire for booty and justified by the ideal of *jihad*. Buddhism suffered greatly from
these raids, since its unfortified monasteries offered easy

pickings. Buddhists were considered 'idolaters' by the Muslims because of the images of Buddhas and bodhisattvas which adorned their monasteries. Works of art were destroyed and libraries burned to the ground. In 1192 a Turkish tribe established rule over north India, the first of a series of Muslim dynasties known as the Delhi Sultanate. The next few centuries would be a time of upheaval and uncertainty, until the Moguls inaugurated an era of relative stability and religious toleration in the sixteenth century. By then, however, it was too late. As if to demonstrate the truth of its own teaching that whatever arises will also cease, Buddhism all but disappeared from the land of its birth.

The history of Buddhism in the rest of Asia can conveniently be discussed in terms of north and south. In general the Mahāyāna form of Buddhism predominates in the north, and the Elder tradition in the south. Since only one of the twelve schools of the Elder tradition survives today, namely the school known as the Theravāda, I will henceforth speak of the two main surviving forms of Buddhism as Mahāyāna and Theravāda.

Sri Lanka

Beginning with the countries to the south, where Theravāda Buddhism predominates, the island of Ceylon—home to the modern state of Sri Lanka—has played a crucial role in preserving and developing Buddhist culture. According to the Buddhist chronicles preserved there, Buddhism was brought to Ceylon in 250 BC by a monk named Mahinda, an envoy of the emperor Ashoka. Mahinda and his fellow monks founded a monastic community at the Mahāvihāra ('Great Monastery') in the capital, Anurādhapura. It was in Sri Lanka some time around 80 BC that the Pali Canon was first written down, as a result of fears that the method of oral transmission would not survive due to warfare and famine.

One of the most famous residents of the island was the Indian monk Buddhaghosa who arrived in the fifth century AD. Buddhaghosa collated and edited the early commentaries on the canon and translated them into Pali. His status and influence may be likened to that of the Christian Church father Saint Augustine (354–430) who lived shortly before him. Buddhaghosa's classic work the *Visuddhimagga* or 'Path of Purification'—a compendium of doctrine and practice—has remained a landmark in Theravāda literature.

From the earliest times Buddhism and politics have been entwined in the country's history, and there has been a close reciprocal relationship between Church and State, or the *Saṅgha* and the king. Kings were consecrated by monks, and monks served as counsellors, interpreting Buddhist teachings for the ruler. Although monks are barred by the present-day constitution from holding political office, they retain considerable influence in public affairs. Buddhism has undergone several periods of decline in the course of its history in Sri Lanka. Often these occurred in the aftermath of invasion—such as by Indian Tamils—or periods of civil unrest. On several occasions the ordination tradition for monks died out, and monks had to be sent for from Burma in 1065 and later Thailand in 1753 in order to restart it. In recent decades the country has been divided by a bitter ethnic feud between the majority Sinhalese population, who are Buddhists, and a minority Tamil population in the north which is mainly Hindu. Buddhism itself, however, continues to flourish, having successfully responded to the challenge of colonialism and adapted to modern democracy.

South-East Asia

Other important Theravāda countries in South-East Asia are Burma (now officially known as Myanmar) and Thailand (formerly Siam). Theravāda Buddhism may have been introduced to this region by one of Ashoka's missions, and it has been present among the native Mon people from the early centuries of the Christian era. South-East Asia has traditionally looked to India for its cultural inspiration, and the influence of both Buddhism and Hinduism has been strong throughout the region. From the fifth to the fifteenth centuries the dominant power in the area was the Khmer empire, in which various forms of Hinduism and Mahāyāna Buddhism were popular. The Burmese chronicles claim that Buddhaghosa visited Burma and established a tradition of Pali scholarship. Various schools of Buddhism flourished until King Anawrahta (1044–77) unified the country by conquering the southern part and gave his allegiance to the Theravāda, although it is likely the Theravāda was dominant even before then. The Mons subsequently recovered their independence and were not finally suppressed until the seventeenth century. Anawrahta's capital, Pagan, was sacked by the Mongols in 1287 and the city with its many thousand pagodas and temples was abandoned. Despite this setback Buddhism recovered and has flourished, and some 85 per cent of the population are now Theravāda Buddhists.

Theravāda had long been established in parts of the neighbouring territory now known as Thailand, notably in the Mon kingdom of Haripuñjaya and the kingdom of Dvāravatī, and in the eleventh century missions were sent from Burma into the region. The Thai people, who arrived in the region in the thirteenth century having been displaced from China by the Mongols, found the Theravāda tradition more congenial than the elaborate Mahāyāna forms of Buddhism they had been familiar with in the north. The Theravāda received royal patronage and before long replaced its rivals. Today it is the official religion of Thailand.

The history of Buddhism in Cambodia, Laos, and Vietnam is not dissimilar, although as one moves further east Theravāda Buddhism progressively gives way to Mahāyāna forms. Much religious syncretism is found in these areas in the form of blends of Theravāda, Mahāyāna, and local indigenous religions. When Buddhism spreads it tends not to eradicate existing beliefs but to incorporate them, along with local gods and spirits, into its own cosmology. It is quite common to find Buddhists at the village level turning to the local gods for solutions to everyday problems—such as curing an illness or finding a marriage partner—and to Buddhism for answers to the larger questions about human destiny.

This pattern of overcoding indigenous beliefs is also found in north Asia where Mahāyāna Buddhism predominates. Mahāyāna Buddhism flourished throughout central Asia, and in Tibet, China, Japan, and Korea. Here I will give only a brief overview of the main developments in China, Japan, and Tibet.

China

Buddhism spread north from India into Central Asia and reached China by the middle of the first century. At this time the later Han Dynasty (206 BC–AD 220) had consolidated Chinese power in Central Asia, and Buddhist monks travelled with caravans which traversed the silk route, the primary artery for the transmission of luxury items from China to the West. To the pragmatic Chinese, Buddhism was both strange and fascinating. The dominant ideology in China was Confucianism, a system of socio-ethical principles deriving from the teachings of the sage K'ung fu-tzu, or Confucius (550–470 BC). On certain matters Buddhism seemed in conflict with Confucian values. Confucianism regarded the family as the foundation of society, and the Buddhist invitation to sons and daughters to leave their families and renounce the world caused it to be seen with the same suspicion as certain cults today. The Buddhist *Saṅgha*, moreover, as a cor-

7. *The Diamond Sūtra*: The world's oldest printed text is a copy of the *Diamond Sūtra*, an important scripture of the Mahāyāna. The copy is dated AD 868.

poration of renunciates, seemed like a state within a state, a challenge to the power of the emperor and a threat to the seamless fabric of social life which was the Confucian ideal. Monks also refused to bow before the emperor, since in India monks were deferred to by laymen. Cultural differences of this kind gave rise to conflict and misunderstanding, and fuelled hostility towards the new religion.

On the other hand there was much about Buddhism that attracted the Chinese. It seemed to take up where Confucianism left off, and described an unseen world about which Confucianism had little to say. A disciple of Confucius once asked, 'Master, how should we treat the spirits and divinities?' The reply was, 'You cannot treat the spirits and divinities properly before you learn to treat your fellow men properly.' When the questioner enquired about death, Confucius gave a similar answer: 'You cannot know about death before you know about life' (*Analects*, xi. 12). In relegating the supernatural to second place, Confucianism left unanswered questions about which many Chinese were curious. Buddhism seemed to have answers to these questions, especially those concerning death and the afterlife, a subject which was of particular interest to the Chinese in view of the deep respect in which ancestors were held. Thus while many Chinese accepted Confucianism as the authoritative guide to this world, they turned to Buddhism for guidance about the next.

Buddhism shared certain similarities with another Chinese philosophy, Taoism, a form of nature-mysticism founded by the legendary sage Lao-tzu (b. 604 BC). The goal of Taoism is to live in harmony with nature by learning to balance the complementary forces of Yin and Yang which are believed to pervade the universe. Yin is the female principle which finds expression in softness and passivity, while Yang is the male principle which manifests itself in hardness and strength. Both these qualities are present in individuals and all phenomena in varying degrees, and the interaction of these forces is what gives rise to change in the world. The sage is one who knows how to keep Yin and Yang in equilibrium and to live in harmony with the changing circumstances of life. A person who could integrate these forces in his own person was thought to gain deep spiritual peace as well as magical powers and longevity. The classic *Tao-te-Ching* or 'Book of the Way and its Virtue', attributed to Lao-tzu, sets out the principles for leading this higher life.

In certain areas Buddhism and Taoism overlapped, and Buddhist meditation seemed geared to the same goal of inner stillness and 'actionless action' (*wu-wei*) sought by the Taoist sage. A school of Chinese Buddhism known as Ch'an (the ancestor of Japanese Zen), was born from this interaction. Yet while Taoist teachings were unsystematic and emphasized quietism and inspiration, Buddhism offered a systematic philosophical framework and a tradition of textual scholarship. This aspect of Buddhism appealed to the Chinese gentry with their love of scholarship and learning, and in due course Buddhism was adopted as the third of the 'three religions' of China, although never quite managing to shake off its foreign associations. A number of Chinese monks made pilgrimages to India in search of manuscripts, notably Fa-hsien (399–413), Hsüan-tsang (630–644) and I-tsing (671–695).

The fortunes of Buddhism in China have waxed and waned over the centuries. It reached its high point under the T'ang dynasty (AD 618–907), although many Tantric masters flourished later during the Mongol period (thirteenth and fourteenth centuries). The arrival of Communism led to the suppression of Buddhism and other forms of religion in the Cultural Revolution of 1966. However, there are now signs of a revival in the People's Republic of China, and Buddhism has remained strong in Taiwan.

Japan

Another important centre of Buddhism in the far east is Japan. Buddhism arrived there in the sixth century by way of Korea, but drew much of its inspiration from mainland China. The Heian period (794–1185) saw the development of schools such as the eclectic Tendai and the esoteric Shingon, both introduced from China. The Pure Land school—a distinctive form of Japanese Buddhism based on devotion to the Buddha Amida—also began to develop around this time and reached its apogee in the Kamakura period (1185–1333).

Nichiren (1222–82) reacted against what he saw as the complacency and escapism of the Pure Land School, and founded a new religious movement which made the *Lotus Sūtra* the centre of cultic practice rather than the Buddha Amida. Instead of reciting the mantra *Namu Amida Butsu* or 'Homage to the Buddha Amida' to ensure rebirth in Amida's paradise, Nichiren's followers recited the mantra *Namu myōhō renge kyō* meaning 'Honour to the *Lotus Sūtra* of the True Dharma'. It was felt that by focusing on these words with faith and devotion, all one's goals—material and spiritual—could be attained. Nichiren sought to institute a programme of socio-religious reform at a national level, and saw a great role for Japan as a centre from which his teachings would spread. To some extent his aims have been realized, and today the words *Namu myōhō renge kyō* are recited daily as part of their religious practice by millions of followers of the Nichiren Shōshū school and its breakaway offshoot, Soka Gakkai International.

In contrast to Indian Buddhism, Japanese Buddhism has a strong social orientation and emphasizes community and group values. Influential teachers such as Shinran (1173–1262) disapproved of monasticism and encouraged monks to marry and play a full part in social life (tradition has it that he practised what he preached, marrying a nun and having five children by her!).

Alongside the Pure Land and Nichiren schools, the third most important school of Japanese Buddhism is Zen, which came to Japan from China (where it was known as Ch'an) and Korea early in the thirteenth century. The word 'Zen' derives from the Sanskrit *dhyāna* (Pali: *jhāna*) meaning 'trance', and meditation plays a central role in Zen practice. Zen holds that enlightenment occurs in a moment of intuitive awakening that is beyond logical comprehension. It observes that these flashes of insight—to which it gives the name *satori*—are often triggered in the course of mundane activity when the mind is calm and relaxed, rather than when engaged in study or intellectual analysis. The experience is likened to the bottom dropping out of a bucket—it happens all of a sudden and quite unexpectedly. Zen compares the unenlightened mind to a pool of muddy water, and argues that the best way to make it clear is to let it be rather than stir

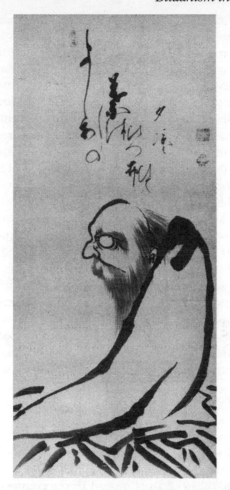

8. *Bodhidharma*: Bodhidharma is credited with having brought the Ch'an form of Buddhism (from which Zen derives) to China early in the sixth century. Legend has it that he spent nine years in meditation facing a wall. The drawing is by Hakuin, who lived in Japan in the eighteenth century. Eisei Bunko, Tokyo

it up through the study of doctrines. Zen has an iconoclastic tendency, and seems to regard the study of texts, doctrines, and dogmas as a potential hindrance to spiritual awakening. Instead, meditation is seen as the best way of achieving mental clarity. Zen also relies on humour, spontaneity, unconventionality, poetry, and other forms of artistic expression to communicate the idea of enlightenment as a supra-rational awakening which can be transmitted from master to student, but which ultimately lies beyond mere 'words and letters'.

Of the two main branches of Zen, the Sōtō school believes that calming meditation is all that is necessary, while Rinzai Zen uses other techniques as a focus of meditation. Most well known is the use of insoluble riddles known as *kō-ans*. A well-known *kō-an* asks, 'What is the sound of one hand clapping?' The Zen master assigns such a riddle to a student to meditate on, and instructs him to return at a certain time with a solution. No rational solution (such as the answer 'silence') is acceptable: what is sought instead is a demonstration that the student has realized that the truth lies beyond rational apprehension. Only when the intellect gives up its restless quest to reduce the Truth to a theory will enlightenment dawn.

Tibet

The final centre of Buddhist culture to be mentioned in this survey is Tibet. Due the difficulties of gaining access to this mountainous region and the absence of established trade routes, Buddhism did not enter Tibet until the eighth century. The form of Buddhism which flourished there is known variously as Tantra, Vajrayāna ('The Vehicle of the Thunderbolt'), or—because of the frequent use it makes of magical formulas and chants—Mantrayāna.

The Vajrayāna adopts Mahāyāna philosophy and cosmology and adds a rich symbolism and set of religious practices

of its own. The core of the movement is a set of arcane treatises known as Tantras, composed in India in the latter part
of the first millennium. The Tantras makes use of mystical
diagrams (*maṇḍalas*) and magic formulas (*mantras*), and are
written in a mysterious 'twilight language' (*sandhyabhāṣā*) to
which only initiates have the key. Initiation is given by a guru
(Tibetan: lama) who then teaches the esoteric meaning of the
words and symbols to his students. In its external forms
Tantra resembles Western schools of ritual magic which
make use of magic circles, pentagrams, spells, and charms.
Based on the view that nirvana and *saṃsāra* are not different, the Tantras teach that anything—even desire—can prof-
itably be used as a means to liberation. The passions come to
be regarded not as inherently wicked but simply as a powerful form of energy which—rather like electricity—can be
used for many purposes. Sexual desire, in particular, formerly regarded as the greatest obstacle to religious progress
for monks, came to be seen as a potent force which, if properly harnessed, could accelerate spiritual development.

Tantric teachings can be understood on various levels.
Some Buddhists formed secret groups—not unlike covens—to
perform rituals of a sexual nature. Others saw the teachings as
allegorical, and not to be taken at face value. Much Tibetan art
and iconography has an explicitly sexual content, but this is
usually interpreted in a symbolic way such that the male partner represents Skilful Means (the various techniques by which
bodhisattvas lead beings to enlightenment) while the female
represents Wisdom: their blissful sexual union is nirvana. The
most influential school of Tibetan Buddhism, the Gelug-pa
founded by Tsong-kha-pa in the fourteenth century, saw
Tantra in the latter way as a vehicle for embodying profound
spiritual truth rather than an invitation to people to overturn
moral norms. The monks of this school, like their early Indian
counterparts, hold strictly to the Monastic Rule which,
amongst its many other requirements, insists on celibacy for

9. *Sand Mandala*: This maṇḍala is made of grains of sand mixed with mineral pigments laid out using a cone-shaped fine-tipped funnel. It takes extreme patience and skill to create, and is destroyed when the ceremony for which it was produced is over. This one was created in Switzerland in 1985.

monks. One school, the Nying-ma-pa ('the Ancients'), however, allows a form of married priesthood.

The Tibetan Dalai Lamas are members of the Gelug-pa school. 'Dalai' is a Mongol word meaning 'ocean' (of wisdom), a title conferred by the Mongol ruler Altan Khan in the sixteenth century. The office of Dalai Lama encompasses both the religious and temporal domains. Tibet was ruled by a series of Dalai Lamas down to modern times, when the present encumbent—the fourteenth Dalai Lama, Tenzin Gyatso—was forced to flee the country in 1959 as a result of Chinese invasion in 1950. Since that time he has resided in Dharamsala, in north-west India. Tibet, meanwhile, has been under Communist control, and a systematic and brutal programme of 'ethnic cleansing' has resulted in the exodus of over a million Tibetan refugees. Many great Buddhist monasteries, with their priceless manuscripts and works of art have been destroyed, although some limited rebuilding of religious sites has taken place from time to time.

The history of Buddhism in Asia and its mode of interaction with other cultures is as fascinating as it is complex. This chapter has attempted to convey merely an impression of the richness and diversity of Buddhism in the Asian continent. The important contributions made by many other Asian cultures, such as Korea, to the historical evolution of Buddhism have been omitted for reasons of space. More detailed studies on the cultures mentioned above will be found in the section on 'Further Reading' at the end.

7 Meditation

*T*he importance of meditation in Buddhism can be appreciated by recalling that it was while meditating that the Buddha gained enlightenment. The image of the Buddha seated cross-legged in meditation (see p. 89) is one of the most popular themes in Buddhist art, and a constant reminder of the close association between meditation and enlightenment. Virtually all schools of Buddhism see meditation as the high road to enlightenment, and it constitutes a major part of the 'experiential' dimension of Buddhism as a religion.

Meditation (*Samādhi*) is one of the three divisions of the Eightfold Path, and thus occupies a central place in Buddhist practice. The more general term for meditation in Buddhism, however, is *bhāvanā*, which means 'cultivation' or literally 'making become'. The literal meaning is quite appropriate, for meditation is the principal Buddhist strategy for making oneself what one wishes to be.

The Indian Background

The meditational techniques in use in the Buddha's day were part of a common spiritual toolkit shared by renouncers

10. *The Buddha meditating*: This massive stone sculpture shows the Buddha meditating in the lotus posture with hands resting in his lap. Amida Buddha, Kamakura, Japan, 13th cent. AD

(*Samaṇas*) and those religious practitioners who followed the orthodox tradition of Indian religion (*Brāhmaṇas*). A few centuries before the Buddha's time, an upsurge of interest in the interior dimension of spiritual life led to the composition of a body of religious literature known as the *Upaniṣads*. These treatises sought to explain the relationship between the inner Self (*ātman*) and the cosmic ground of being, and described mystical techniques by which the Self could realize its identity with that highest reality (*Brahman*). Although the Buddha disagreed with the underlying philosophy of these texts, he was none the less in sympathy with their message that salvation must be sought within, and could only come through a deep understanding of one's nature.

In addition to the teachings of the *Upaniṣads*, the Buddha would also have been familiar with the beliefs and practices of the Yoga tradition. Although basing themselves on philosophical teachings which the Buddha rejected, practitioners of yoga developed a sophisticated set of techniques for disciplining both the mind and body. Yoga is related to the English word 'yoke', and yoga practice involves a sophisticated spiritual technology for yoking and harnessing the powers of the mind. Most readers will be familiar with the various physical exercises and postures of yoga, the purpose of which is to make the body supple, pliant, and healthy. The techniques of meditation used in yoga do roughly the same thing for the mind, providing a comprehensive tune-up kit for peak mental functioning. The Buddha thus did not invent meditation, but, as we shall see below, he did introduce significant modifications to the methods of his contemporaries which makes Buddhist meditation distinctive in both theory and practice.

The Nature of Meditation

But what exactly *is* meditation? Meditation may be defined as an altered state of consciousness which is induced in a controlled manner. There is nothing very mysterious about it, and people slip in and out of trance-like states akin to meditation spontaneously in the course of waking life. A good deal of waking life is punctuated by daydreams, reveries, and fantasies in which the mind withdraws to contemplate an interior landscape. Sometimes these reveries can be quite absorbing, as when driving a car one suddenly finds oneself at the destination with very little recollection of the trip. Taking drugs may also produce effects not unlike those experienced in meditation.

The main differences between meditation and the states mentioned above are the degree of control exercised and the depth and duration of the experience. Also—unlike drugs— with meditation there are no side effects or 'bad trips', and the benefits are cumulative and sustained. In the normal waking state the mind meanders in and out of trance-states continually. Someone interrupted in the course of a reverie may remark that his mind was 'elsewhere'. The goal of meditation is not to be 'elsewhere' but to be right here, fully conscious and aware. The aim is to 'get one's head together', and become mentally concentrated rather than fragmented. A laser beam provides a good analogy: when light is diffuse it is relatively powerless, but when focused and concentrated it can cut through steel. Or, to use sound as a metaphor rather than light, the aim of meditation is to screen out mental 'static' and reduce the mental 'chatter' which dissipates psychic energy.

The Practice of Meditation

Meditational theory recognizes a close relationship between body and mind, so before the mind can become completely calm the body must be composed. The traditional posture for meditation is to sit cross-legged, using a cushion if necessary, with the back straight, head slightly inclined, and hands resting in the lap. This is known as the 'lotus posture' (the Buddha is depicted in this posture on p. 89). Although it may feel unnatural at first to a beginner, with a little practice this position can be held for long periods of time. It allows the meditator to breathe in a deep and relaxed way and to remain comfortable but alert. Meditation can be performed in any position which is comfortable, but if the position is too comfortable there is a risk of falling asleep. Control of the mind when asleep is obviously very difficult, although there is a Tibetan practice known as 'dream yoga' in which awareness is cultivated during lucid dreams.

Once a comfortable posture has been established a suitable object for meditation is chosen. When the Buddha left home he studied separately with two teachers of meditation, and it can reasonably be assumed that what they taught him—namely how to enter and abide in a deep state of trance—was typical of the meditation practised at the time. What instructions would the Buddha's two teachers have given to their student? We cannot know for sure, but they may have advised him to concentrate on his breathing, or to repeat a *mantra* silently to himself. Alternatively, they might have placed an object a few feet away—perhaps a small everyday item such as a pot or a flower—and instructed him to study it carefully, noting every detail until he could recreate a perfect mental image of the object with his eyes closed. The object of these exercises is for the mind to become completely engrossed in the object until the awareness of subject and object dissolves in a unified field of consciousness.

Meditation is by no means easy to master, since the mind continually throws up distractions. Buddhist sources compare the mind to a monkey which swings through the trees, taking hold of one branch after another. The reader may wish to put this to the test by concentrating on one of the illustrations in this book, such as the sand *maṇḍala* on p. 86, and noting how little time it takes for the mind to become restless and move elsewhere. Firm and steady concentration comes only with regular practice and it normally takes several months before results are achieved. Learning to meditate is a bit like learning to play a musical instrument: it requires determination, commitment, and daily practice.

Results eventually manifest themselves in the form of

	Level of Trance	Characteristics	
	The Attainment of Cessation	'Touching Nirvana with the Body'	
Sphere of Formlessness	8th *Jhāna*	Neither perception nor non-perception	
	7th *Jhāna*	Nothingness	
	6th *Jhāna*	Infinite Consciousness	
	5th *Jhāna*	Infinite Space	
Sphere of Pure Form	4th *Jhāna*	Concentration Equanimity 'Beyond pleasure and pain'	Psychic powers attained at this stage
	3th *Jhāna*	Concentration Equanimity	Clairvoyance Clairaudience Retrocognition
	2nd *Jhāna*	Concentration Rapture Joy	Telepathy Psychokinesis
	1st *Jhāna*	Discursive thought Detachment Rapture Joy	

The Eight Stages of Trance (jhāna)

heightened powers of concentration and an increasing sense of calm and inner stillness, which is carried over into everyday life. Distractions, worries, doubts, and fears lose their hold over the mind, and the meditator becomes generally more 'together', living more fully in the here and now.

Meditators who are particularly adept may eventually achieve a lucid state of rapt absorption known as *samādhi*, a condition of complete and unwavering inner stillness. Under his teachers the Buddha was able to achieve two particularly lofty states of this kind, which subsequently became incorporated into the formal Buddhist meditational framework as the seventh and eighth *jhānas*.

The jhānas

The basis of this framework are the *jhānas* (Sanskrit: *dhyāna*) or levels of trance. In the first and lowest *jhāna*, the mind thinks discursively but is filled with detachment, rapture, and joy. In the second *jhāna*, discursive thought falls away and is replaced by absorption (*samādhi*) and a heightened sense of awareness. In the third *jhāna*, rapture is replaced by equanimity, and in the fourth even equanimity gives way to a state described as 'beyond pleasure and pain'. These mystical experiences seem to transcend linguistic categories, and it is not easy to find the appropriate vocabulary to describe them. It can be seen, however, that the trend is for the higher states of trance to be increasingly subtle and sublime, and for the grosser, more emotional, elements such as excitement and rapture to be replaced by a deeper and more refined absorption. This leads to a condition called 'one-pointedness' (*ekaggatā*) in which the mind remains fixed exclusively on the object of meditation in the laser-like manner referred to above.

In the fourth *jhāna* the meditator can develop various psychic powers corresponding roughly to what in the West is known as extra-sensory perception (ESP). These include the power to see events occurring in remote places (clairvoyance), to hear distant sounds (clairaudience), to recall previous lives (retrocognition), and to know the thoughts of others (telepathy). A collection of miscellaneous psychokinetic powers are also acquired such as the ability to fly through the air, walk on water, and create duplicate bodies. There is nothing distinctly Buddhist about these abilities and they are widely acknowledged in Indian thought as attainable by anyone wishing to invest the necessary time and effort. Although the Buddha is said to have possessed these abilities himself, he sometimes mocked those who went to great lengths to acquire them, pointing out that rather than devote years of one's life to learning to walk on water it was simpler to engage the services of a boatman!

During the deeper stages of meditation the main bodily functions become subdued, and breathing is all but suspended. Research suggests that the brain generates more alpha-waves in this state, indicating a condition of relaxed creativity. Many unusual sensations may occur: perceptions of light are common along with a feeling of floating or lightness in the limbs. At the deeper levels of trance, it is said that the natural purity of the mind, normally screened by the static of waking consciousness, manifests itself in its full radiance. The mind in this condition is likened to purified gold in the malleable and pliable state from which precious objects are formed by a skilful artisan. In this case the artisan is the meditator who, having access to the deep levels of the psyche, is equipped to undertake the task of remodelling himself.

Later literature provides a list of forty meditation subjects. To choose the right object requires skill and discrimination, and a teacher is invaluable in assessing the personality of the student and finding the right subject to suit his or her personality and spiritual needs. For example, someone who is attached to bodily pleasure might be instructed to meditate on the body as impermanent, subject to old age and sickness, and full of impurities, in order to weaken attachment to it. A person of simple piety, on the other hand, might be instructed to meditate on the Buddha and his virtues, or on the 'Three Jewels', namely the Buddha, the Dharma, and the Saṅgha. There are also more gruesome subjects, such as the charred and dismembered bodies seen in the cremation ground. The purpose of this meditation is to come face to face with death and realize how urgent it is to make the best use of the precious opportunities which human rebirth has bestowed.

The Four Measureless States

Among the most popular meditation subjects are the four 'Measureless States', (*Brahma-vihāra*) namely loving-kindness (*mettā*), compassion (*karuṇā*), sympathetic joy (*muditā*), and equanimity (*upekkhā*). The practice of loving-kindness involves developing an attitude of benevolence, friendship, and goodwill towards all living creatures. The meditator begins with himself as the object of goodwill. This requirement is not narcissistic, and is based on the shrewd observation that a person is only capable of loving others to the extent that he is capable of loving himself. Someone affected by low self-esteem or consumed by self-loathing will not be capable of loving others fully. The meditator reviews his good and bad points as objectively as possible while keeping in mind the thought 'may I be happy and free from suffering'. He then gradually extends the circle of benevolence to others 'like a skilled ploughman marks out his territory and then covers it', incorporating his family, the neighbourhood, town, state, nation, and in due course all the creatures in the six directions. At every opportunity he recalls deeds of kindness done to him by others, even in past lives. The cultivation of this universal goodwill frees the mind from partiality and prejudice, and the meditator begins to act towards others with kindness and without discrimination. The remaining three Measureless States are cultivated in a similar way. Through compassion the meditator identifies with the suffering of others, and through sympathetic joy he rejoices in their happiness and good fortune. The cultivation of equanimity ensures that these dispositions are always balanced and appropriate to the circumstances.

Meditation and Cosmology

In the tripartite division of the Buddhist universe, made up of the sphere of sense-desires, the sphere of pure form, and the sphere of formlessness, the topography of the spiritual and material worlds overlap. Within this scheme the human world and the lower heavens are found at the bottom within the sphere of sense-desires, while the four *jhānas* just considered are mapped to second level, the sphere of pure form. The gods who dwell in the various levels of the sphere of pure form thus abide in the same state of mind as the meditator in the corresponding *jhāna*. The corollary of this is that meditation provides an experience of heaven. To the basic scheme of four *jhānas* another four were added and mapped to the sphere of formlessness. These four higher or 'formless' *jhānas* (so-called because being in the formless realm they have an object which is totally mental, beyond all form) correspond to the four highest cosmological planes in which rebirth can take place.

The final Buddhist scheme of meditational cosmology thus consists of the eight *jhānas* which are located in the top two-thirds of the cosmos. Under his first teacher the Buddha attained the seventh, and under his second teacher the eighth and highest. A ninth stage known as the 'attainment of cessation' (*nirodha-samāpatti*) is also mentioned in some sources. In this stage all mental operations are completely suspended, and even heartbeat and respiration cease. Life subsists simply in the form of residual bodily heat. A person can, we are told, remain in this state for several days, eventually emerging from it spontaneously at a predetermined time. This condition is held to be the closest anyone can come to experiencing final nirvana while still alive, and is described as 'touching nirvana with the body'.

Insight Meditation (vipassanā)

If meditation is such a powerful technique, why did the Buddha turn his back on his teachers? The Buddha's reason for leaving was that he came to see that entering into a state of trance, however blissful and serene, was only a temporary diversion and not a permanent solution to suffering. Meditational states, like everything else in saṃsāra, are impermanent and do not last. What these teachers and their meditational techniques failed to provide was the kind of deep philosophical insight into the nature of things which is needed for complete liberation.

The Buddha, therefore, developed a completely new meditational technique to supplement the practices he learned from his teachers. To the kind of techniques already described, which in Buddhism go by the generic name of 'calming meditation' (samatha), the Buddha added a new one called 'insight meditation' (vipassanā). The goal of this was not peace and tranquillity but the generation of penetrating and critical insight (paññā). Whereas in calming meditation intellectual activity subsides at an early stage (on reaching the second jhāna), in insight meditation the object of the exercise is to bring the critical faculties fully into play in a detailed reflexive analysis of the meditator's own state of mind. In practice, the two techniques of calming and insight are normally used back-to-back within the same session: calming may be used first to concentrate the mind and then insight to probe and analyse. It is impossible to practise insight meditation without having reached at least the level of calm of the first jhāna.

In insight meditation, the meditator examines every

aspect of his subjective experience, breaking this down into four categories: the body and its physical sensations; feelings; mood; and mental patterns and thoughts. A typical session might proceed by extending awareness of the rise and fall of the breath to the rest of the body. Every minor sensation would be noted such as twinges, aches, itches and the impulse to move and scratch. The meditator does not respond to these impulses since the purpose of the exercise is to note with bare attention how bodily sensations arise and subside without reacting to them in the normal semi-automatic way. By learning to observe without becoming involved, the pattern of stimulus–response which underlies much human behaviour can be broken. Little by little the realization dawns that one is free to choose how to react in all situations regardless which buttons are pushed. The grip of long-standing habits and compulsions is weakened and replaced with a new sense of freedom. The analysis is gradually extended to the whole body, the intellect being wielded like a surgeon's scalpel to dissect the various bodily parts and functions. From this the awareness arises that the body is nothing more than a temporary assemblage of bones, nerves, and tissues, certainly not a worthy object to become infatuated with or excessively attached to.

Next, attention is directed to whatever feelings arise. Pleasant and unpleasant feelings are noted as they arise and pass away. This sharpens the perception of impermanence and gives rise to the knowledge that even those things which seem most intimate to us—such as our emotions—are transient states which come and go. Next, the subject's current mood and the constant fluctuations in its overall quality and tone are observed, and finally the stream of thoughts which passes through the mind. The meditator must resist the temptation to lose himself in the daydreams and fantasies which inevitably arise. Instead, he simply observes with detachment as the thoughts and images follow one another, regarding them like clouds passing across a clear blue sky, or bubbles floating to the top of a glass. From this detached observation it gradually becomes clear that even one's conscious mind is but a process like everything else. Most people regard their mental life as their true inner essence (one thinks of Descartes's famous statement 'I think therefore I am'), but insight meditation discloses that the stream of consciousness is just one more facet of the complex interaction of the five factors of individuality, and not what one 'really is'.

The realization that there is no hidden subject who is the owner of these various sensations, feelings, moods, and ideas, and that all that exists are the experiences themselves, is the transformative insight which triggers enlightenment. The recognition that there is ultimately no subject that 'has' desires weakens and finally destroys craving once and for all, making it 'like a palm tree whose roots have been destroyed, never to grow again'. Experientially, it is as if a great burden has been lifted: the clamourings of the ego, with its vanities, illusions, cravings, and disappointments, are silenced. The result is not some kind of Stoic passivity, for emotion is not suppressed but merely freed from the distorting gravitational pull of the ego. Others begin to come more fully within one's emotional horizon as the merry-go-round of selfish craving and gratification slows and stops, to be replaced by a deep and lasting sense of peace and contentment.

Summary

Meditation is of great importance and is central to the practice of the Eightfold Path. Through the cultivation of attitudes such as benevolence, using the techniques of calming meditation, a deep moral concern for others is fostered. Based on this concern one begins to act spontaneously for their welfare and to place their interests on a par with one's own. The Buddhist version of the Golden Rule advises: 'Since all beings seek happiness and shun suffering, one should never do anything to that one would not like to be done to oneself.' By acting in accordance with principles of this kind one becomes perfect in Virtue (*sīla*). By cultivating analytical understanding, through insight meditation, Wisdom (*paññā*) arises, and one comes to understand the Truth of Suffering, the Truth of Arising, the Truth of Cessation, and the Truth of the Path.

The three components of the Eightfold Path—Morality, Meditation, and Wisdom—are thus like the three sides of a triangle. Meditation, however, is not just a *means* to Virtue and Wisdom: it if were, it would be merely a technique which can be discarded once they had been attained. Since the Buddha continued to practise meditation even after his enlightenment it can safely be concluded that the states experienced in meditation are intrinsically valuable human experiences. An analogy can be drawn with swimming: a person learns to swim *by* swimming, but then rather than stop, swims for the sheer satisfaction and well-being that the exercise provides.

8 Ethics

Dharma

Morality (*sīla*) is the first of the three divisions of the Eightfold Path and the foundation of the religious life. Moral development is a prerequisite for the cultivation of Meditation (*samādhi*) and Wisdom (*paññā*). To live a moral life is to live in accordance with Dharma. The term 'Dharma' has many meanings, but the underlying idea is of a universal law which governs both the physical and moral order of the universe. Dharma is neither caused by nor under the control of a supreme being, and the gods themselves are subject to its laws. In Buddhism the term is used to denote both the natural order, and—as already noted—the entire corpus of Buddhist ethico-religious teachings. There is felt to be a correspondence between the two in the sense that Buddhist teachings are thought to be objectively true and in accordance with the nature of things.

Dharma may be translated as 'Natural Law', a term which captures both its main senses, namely as the principle of order and regularity seen in the behaviour of natural phenomena, and also the idea of a universal moral law whose requirements have been discovered by enlightened beings such as the Buddha (note that the Buddha discovered

Dharma, he did not invent it). Every aspect of life is regulated by Dharma; the physical laws which regulate the rising of the sun, the succession of the seasons, the movement of the constellations. In the moral order, Dharma is manifest in the law of karma, which governs the way moral deeds affect individuals in present and future lives. Living in accordance with Dharma and implementing its requirements leads to happiness, fulfilment and salvation; neglecting or transgressing against it leads to endless suffering in the cycle of rebirth (*saṃsāra*).

In common with Indian moral tradition as a whole, Buddhism expresses its ethical requirements in the form of duties. The most general moral duties are those found in the Five Precepts, such as the duty to refrain from killing, stealing, and so forth (see text box overleaf). These apply to everyone without exception. On becoming a Buddhist one formally 'takes' (or accepts) the precepts in a ritual context, and the form of words used acknowledges the free and voluntary assumption of the duty assumed.

Virtues

Although the precepts are of great importance in Buddhist morality, there is more to the moral life than following rules. Rules must not just be followed, but followed for the right reasons and with the correct motivation. It is here that the role of the virtues becomes important, and Buddhist morality as a whole may be likened to a coin with two faces: on one side are the precepts and on the other the virtues. The precepts, in fact, may be thought of simply as a list of things which a virtuous person will never do.

Early sources emphasize the importance of cultivating correct dispositions and habits so that moral conduct becomes the natural and spontaneous manifestation of internalized and properly integrated beliefs and values,

Buddhist Precepts

There are five main sets of precepts in Buddhism:

1. The Five Precepts (*pañcasīla*)
2. The Eight Precepts (*aṭṭhaṅgasīla*)
3. The Ten Precepts (*dasasīla*)
4. The Ten Good Paths of Action (*dasakusalakamma-patha*)
5. The Monastic Disciplinary Code (*pātimokkha*)

The most widely observed of these codes is the first, the Five Precepts for laymen. The Five Precepts forbid (1) killing, (2) stealing, (3) sexual immorality, (4) lying, and (5) taking intoxicants. The core of Buddhist morality is contained in the first four. These are supplemented by more rigorous precepts according to the status of the practitioner or to suit particular ceremonial occasions. The fifth precept, against taking intoxicants, for example, is thought to be particularly relevant for layfolk, while the Eight and Ten precepts, which supplement the basic five with additional restrictions such as on the time when meals may be taken, are commonly adopted as additional commitments on holy days (*uposatha*). The Monastic Disciplinary Code (*pātimokkha*) contained in the Monastic Rule (*vinaya*) is a set of over two hundred rules (the exact number varies slightly between schools) which set out in detail the regulations for communal monastic life.

rather than simple conformity to external rules. Many formulations of the precepts make this clear. Of someone who follows the First Precept it is said in the texts, 'Laying aside the cudgel and the sword he dwells compassionate and kind to all living creatures' (D.i.4). Abstention from taking life is therefore ideally the result of a compassionate identification with living things, rather than a constraint which is imposed contrary to natural inclination. To observe the first precept perfectly requires a profound understanding of the relationship between living things (according to Buddhism, in the long cycle of reincarnation we have all been each others' fathers, mothers, son, etc.) coupled with an unswerving disposition of universal benevolence and compassion. Although few have perfected these capacities, in respecting the precepts they habituate themselves to the condition of one who has, and in so doing come a step closer to enlightenment.

The virtues, as Aristotle, points out, are about what is difficult. The task of the virtues is to counteract negative dispositions (or vices) such as pride and selfishness. The lengthy lists of virtues and vices which appear in later literature are extrapolated from a key cluster of three virtues, the three Buddhist 'Cardinal Virtues' of non-attachment (*arāga*), benevolence (*adosa*), and understanding (*amoha*). These are the opposites of the three 'roots of evil' mentioned in earlier chapters, namely greed (*rāga*), hatred (*dosa*), and delusion (*moha*). Non-attachment means the absence of that selfish desire which taints moral behaviour by allocating a privileged status to one's own needs. Benevolence means an attitude of goodwill to all living creatures, and understanding means knowledge of human nature and human good as set out in doctrines such as the Four Noble Truths.

Ahiṃsā, *or the inviolability of life*

The cornerstone of Buddhist ethics is its belief in the inviolability of life. This ideal was promoted vigorously by the unorthodox renouncer (*samaṇa*) movements such as Buddhism and Jainism (a renouncer tradition similar to Buddhism in certain respects and founded slightly earlier), but increasingly influenced orthodox schools. Animal sacrifice, which had played an important part in religious rites in India from ancient times, was rejected by both Buddhism and Jainism as cruel and barbaric. Due in part to their influence, blood sacrifices in the orthodox Brahmanical tradition came increasingly to be replaced by symbolic offerings such as vegetables, fruit, and milk.

Among the renouncers, the principle of the sanctity of life, or *ahiṃsā*, was sometimes taken to extremes. Jain monks, for example, took the greatest precautions against destroying tiny forms of life such as insects, even unintentionally. Their practices had some influence on Buddhism, and Buddhist monks often used a strainer to make sure they did not destroy small creatures in their drinking-water. They also avoided travel during the monsoon to avoid treading on insects and other small creatures which became abundant after the rains. In some Buddhist cultures the practice of agriculture is frowned upon because of the inevitable destruction of life caused by ploughing the earth. In general, however, although Buddhism shared the traditional Indian (and Indo-European) view of the sanctity of life, it regarded the destruction of life as morally wrong only when it was caused intentionally or as a result of negligence.

Abortion

How do Buddhist ethical teachings like *ahiṃsā* affect its approach to contemporary moral dilemmas such as abortion? Is Buddhism 'pro-life' or 'pro-choice'? The Buddhist belief in rebirth clearly introduces a new dimension to the abortion debate. For one thing, it puts the question 'When does life begin?'—a key question in the context of abortion—in an entirely new light. For Buddhism, life is a continuum with no discernible starting point. Birth and death are like a revolving door through which an individual passes again and again. But does belief in rebirth increase or reduce the seriousness of abortion? It may be thought that it reduces it, since all that has been done is to postpone rebirth to a later time. Traditional sources, however, do not take this view, and regard the intentional killing of a human being at any stage of life as wrong, regardless of the fact that he or she will be born again.

Although in one sense life is a continuum, Buddhism also believes that each life as an embodied individual (one's existence this time as George or Georgina) has a clear beginning and end. From the earliest times Buddhist sources have been quite clear that individual human life begins at conception, a view widely shared in contemporary Buddhist societies. The ancient authorities, of course, had an imperfect knowledge of embryology, particularly concerning conception, but their understanding of foetal development as a gradual process with a definite starting point was not very different to that of modern science. Interpreting the early sources in the light of modern scientific discoveries such as ovulation, most Buddhists have arrived at the conclusion that individual life begins at fertilization, the moment when the sperm and ovum come together. Because of this, in the more traditional Buddhist countries such as Sri Lanka and Thailand, abortion is illegal with certain limited exceptions, such as when necessary to save the mother's life. Elsewhere in Asia practice varies. In Japan (where Buddhism has been influential but is not the state religion), abortion is legal and around a million abortions are performed each year. This compares with a figure of 1.5 million for the United States, a country with over twice the population of Japan. The annual total for the United Kingdom is around 180,000.

While recognizing that abortion means taking life, Buddhism is also renowned for its benevolence, toleration, and compassion. Some contemporary Buddhists, especially in the West, feel that there is more to be said on the matter than is found in the ancient sources, and that there may be circumstances in which abortion may be justified. For one thing, early Buddhist attitudes were formulated in a society which took a very different view of the status of women from that of the modern West. Feminist writers have drawn attention to the patriarchal nature of traditional societies and to the institutionalized repression of women down the centuries (others deny that either of these historical claims is correct, except at specific times and places). It has also been argued that abortion rights are integral to the emancipation of women and are necessary to redress injustice. Buddhists who are sympathetic to this view and who support the notion of the woman's 'right to choose' may recommend meditation and discussion with a Buddhist teacher as ways in which the woman can get in touch with her feelings and come to a decision in harmony with her conscience.

A constructive contribution to the dilemma posed by abortion has been evolved in recent decades by Japanese Buddhists. The problem of abortion in Japan is particularly acute because the contraceptive pill has not been widely available, apparently because of concerns about side effects. In the absence of effective prevention an efficient (and profitable) abortion industry has emerged to deal with the problem of unwanted pregnancies. Faced with the pain and anguish these situations create, Japanese society has searched its ancient cultural heritage and evolved a unique solution, in the form of the *mizuko kuyō* memorial service for aborted children.

The service is generally a simple one in which a small figure of the bodhisattva Jizō represents the departed child. Often the image is decorated with a child's bib, and toys are placed alongside (see p. 109). Traditionally the image would be placed in the home or at a small roadside shrine, but in recent years specialist temples have appeared which offer commemorative services of various degrees of sophistication. The ceremony can take many forms, but would typically involve the parents, and sometimes other members of the family, paying their respects to the image by bowing, lighting a candle, and perhaps reciting a Buddhist *sūtra*. The

11. Statues of the bodhisattva Jizō representing aborted children:
Hasedera Temple, Kanagawa Prefecture, Japan

rite may be repeated at intervals such as on the anniversary
of the abortion. The public nature of the ceremonial simultaneously acknowledges the child that has been lost and
helps those involved come to terms with the event on an
emotional level. Some Western clergy have shown interest in
following the Japanese example developing a Christian version of the *mizuko kuyō* ritual for use in churches in the
West. Perhaps this is an indication of the way in which
Buddhism is already beginning to influence Western culture.

Rights

While duties have been mentioned, nothing has so far been
said about rights. Slogans such as the 'right to choose', 'the

right to life', and (in the context of euthanasia) the 'right to die', are the common currency of contemporary debate. However, there is no word in early Buddhist sources corresponding to the notion of 'rights' in the way understood in the West. The concept of a right emerged in the West as the result of a particular combination of social, political, and intellectual developments which have not been repeated elsewhere. From the Enlightenment in the eighteenth century, it has occupied centre-stage in legal and political discourse, and provides a supple and flexible language in terms of which individuals may express their claims to justice. A right may be defined as an exercisable power vested in an individual. This power may be thought of as a benefit or entitlement, which allows the right-holder to impose a claim upon others or to remain immune from demands which others seek to impose.

If Buddhism has no concept of rights, how appropriate is it for Buddhists to use the language of rights when discussing moral issues? A Buddhist may argue that the discourse of rights is not inappropriate for Buddhism because rights and duties are related. A right can be regarded as the converse of a duty. If *A* has a duty to *B*, then *B* stands in the position of beneficiary and has a *right* to whatever benefit flows from the performance of his duty on the part of *A*. Although rights are not explicitly mentioned in Buddhist sources, it may be thought that they are implicit in the notion of dharmic duties. If a king has a duty to rule justly, then it can be said that citizens have a 'right' to fair treatment. At a more general level, if everyone has a duty not to take life, then living creatures have a right to life; if everyone has a duty not to steal, then everyone has a right not to be unjustly deprived of their property. Thus it might be argued that the concept of rights is implicit in Dharma, and that rights and duties are like separate windows onto the common good of justice.

Human Rights

Contemporary human rights charters, such as the United Nations Universal Declaration on Human Rights of 1948, set out a list of basic rights which are held to be possessed by all human beings without distinction as to race or creed. Many Buddhists subscribe to such Charters, and Buddhist leaders such as the Dalai Lama can often be heard endorsing the principles these charters embody. Certain of these rights seem to be foreshadowed in Buddhist sources: a right not to be held in slavery can be found in the canonical prohibition on trade in living beings (A.iii.208). It is also arguable that other human rights are implicit in the Buddhist precepts. The right not to be killed or tortured, for example, may be thought of as implicit in the First Precept.

On the whole, however, traditional sources have little to say about the kinds of questions which are now regarded as human rights issues. In the absence of an explicit concept of rights, of course, this is not unexpected, but Buddhism must provide some account of how the idea of human rights can be grounded in Buddhist doctrine. How might it do this? It might begin by pointing out that human rights are closely tied to the notion of human dignity. Many human rights charters, in fact, explicitly derive the former from the latter. In many religions human dignity is said to derive from the fact that human beings are created in the image of God. Buddhism, of course, makes no such claim. This makes it difficult to see what the source of human dignity might be. If it is not to be sought at a theological level, it must be sought at the human level. In Buddhism, it seems that human dignity flows from the capacity of human beings to gain enlightenment, as demonstrated by the historical figure of the Buddha and the saints of the Buddhist tradition. A Buddha is a living celebration of human potential, and it is in the profound knowledge and compassion which he exemplifies—

qualities which all human beings can emulate—that human dignity may be found. Buddhism teaches that we are all potential Buddhas (some Mahāyāna schools express this by saying that all beings possess the 'Buddha-nature' or the seed of enlightenment). By virtue of this common potential for enlightenment, all individuals are worthy of respect, and justice therefore demands that the rights of each individual must be protected.

Monastic Ethics

The life of a Buddhist monk or nun is regulated by the Monastic Rule (*vinaya*). The Monastic Rule is part of the Pali Canon and is a compendium of information about all aspects of the monastic Order. It describes its origins and history, the early councils, disputes over matters of monastic conduct, and recounts how the traditions of the order arose. Embedded in the Monastic Rule is a code of 227 articles known as the *Pātimokkha* which provide detailed instructions as to how monks should live communally. In many respects the Monastic Rule is comparable to the Rule of St Benedict, which was introduced in the sixth century as a model for the daily life of Christian monks. The Monastic Rule, however, is much longer than the Rule of St Benedict. Amongst other things it provides an account of the circumstances as to why each rule was introduced, and of modifications which were made as new circumstances arose. The Buddha is represented as the author of the rules, although internal evidence suggests that many of them date from some time after his death. Much technical information is provided concerning the types of robes to be worn, the way dwellings should be constructed, how high beds should be off the floor, the type of mats to be used, and so on.

As well as much intricate detail on daily life, however, the Monastic Rule incorporates the major moral precepts such as those against taking life, stealing, and lying. The records of particular offences under these rubrics, moreover, are a vitally important source of information from an ethical perspective. Many of the case-histories reported shed much-needed light on the ethical principles which underlie the rules themselves. Whereas in the Buddha's discourses moral rules are commonly presented in summary form with little explanation, in the Monastic Rule it is possible to discern more clearly the nature of the wrong that is done. The commentaries and discussions concerning the interpretation of the monastic rules is the closest Buddhism comes to the discipline of moral philosophy, and provides a much-needed source of clarification on many points of ethics.

The various monastic precepts mentioned above may therefore be regarded as a combination of *moral* precepts with additional practices designed to cultivate restraint and self-discipline. The large number of monastic rules ensures standardization and conformity within monastic communities, such that disputes and disagreements are kept to a minimum and the Order presents itself as a moral microcosm for the world at large.

Skilful Means

An important innovation in Mahāyāna ethics was the doctrine of skilful means (*upāya-kauśalya*). The roots of this idea are found in the Buddha's skill in teaching the Dharma, demonstrated in his ability to adapt his message to the context in which it was delivered. For example, when talking to Brahmins the Buddha would often explain his teachings by reference to their rituals and traditions, leading his audience step by step to see the truth of a Buddhist tenet. Parables, metaphors, and similes formed an important part of his teaching repertoire, skilfully tailored to suit the level of his audience.

The Mahāyāna developed this idea in a radical way by intimating, in texts such as the *Lotus Sūtra*, that the early teachings were not just skilfully delivered, but were a 'skilful means' (*upāya*) in their entirety. This idea has certain implications for ethics. If the early teachings were provisional rather than ultimate, then the precepts they contain would also be of a provisional rather than an ultimate nature. Thus the clear and strict rules encountered again and again in the early sources which prohibit certain sorts of acts could be interpreted more in the way of guidelines for those at a preliminary stage, but not as ultimately binding. In particular, bodhisattvas, the new moral heroes of the Mahāyāna, could claim increased moral latitude and flexibility based on their recognition of the importance of compassion. A bodhisattva takes a vow to save all beings, and there is evidence in many texts of impatience with rules and regulations which seem to get in the way of a bodhisattva going about his mission. The pressure to bend or suspend the rules in the interests of compassion results in certain texts establishing new codes of conduct for bodhisattvas which sometimes allow the precepts to be broken. In the more extreme of these, even killing is said to be justified to prevent someone committing a heinous crime (such as killing an enlightened person) for which the killer would suffer karmic retribution. Telling lies, and other breaches of the precept, are also said to be permissible in exceptional circumstances.

It is not always clear, however, to what extent this 'new morality' is a departure from the traditional view. For example, if killing an assailant is the only way to prevent him committing murder, it is arguable that such an act is not against the First Precept. As always, intention is paramount. What is intended in such a case may be to neutralize the attack, not to cause the assailant's death. So long as the degree of force used is the minimum necessary to restrain the assailant, even lethal force may be justified as a last resort if the intention is to protect life rather than destroy it. In other cases where the newer 'situational' approach would lead to a clear breach of the precepts there is not much evidence of support from other sources. In general the view of both the early and later tradition is that the major moral precepts—such as those against killing, stealing, lying, and sexual immorality—express requirements of Dharma which are as universal and absolute as the obligations set forth in human rights charters.

The ethical and legal dimension of Buddhism is likely to become increasingly important as Buddhism spreads in the West. How it adapts to, and influences, Western ethics and law will be one of the most fascinating aspects of the contemporary cultural encounter which is the subject of the next chapter.

9 Buddhism in the West

Early Contacts

Although Buddhism spread throughout Asia it remained virtually unknown in the West until modern times. The early missions sent by the emperor Ashoka to the West did not bear fruit, and Western visitors to ancient India left few traces in history.

Alexander the Great's military campaign in Asia in the fourth century BC took him as far as the river Indus, in present-day Pakistan. Alexander crossed the Indus in 326 BC but then turned back westward and died in Babylon not long after, in 323 BC. The heir to the eastern part of Alexander's empire, Seleucus Nikator, soon found himself in conflict with the Mauryan dynasty (321 BC–184 BC) in India. Eventually, in 303 BC, a peace treaty was agreed, and a Greek ambassador by the name of Megasthenes visited the court of Chandragupta Maurya, the grandfather of Ashoka, at the Mauryan capital, Pāṭaliputta (modern Patna). Following these initial contacts, tales of the holy men of India, known to the Greeks as 'gymnophysists', began to circulate in the Hellenic world. Detailed information about Indian religion, however, was sparse, and for the most part the talk was of marvels such as men who walked with their heads under one arm. Buddhism, therefore, remained virtually unknown to the classical world.

In the thirteenth century, Marco Polo travelled through central Asia to China, and his journey brought him into contact with the Mahāyāna form of Buddhism. Of the Buddha he wrote: 'But it is certain, had he been baptized a Christian, he would have been a great saint alongside Our Lord Jesus Christ.' Around the same time, the tale of *Barlaam and Josephaat* became one of the most popular stories of the Middle Ages: although its medieval readers would not have known, the tale is based on a life of the Buddha composed in India around a thousand years earlier. Josephaat is a corruption of the word 'bodhisattva'.

It was not until the Portuguese discovered a sea route to India in 1498 that the possibility for sustained contact between East and West arose. The residents of the prosperous empires of Asia, however, had little interest in Europeans or the remote and sparsely populated continent from which they came. For their part, the first European visitors to Asia were more intent on finding gold or making converts to Christianity than in studying 'heathen' religions. Although the Jesuits who encountered Buddhism in China and Japan from the sixteenth century were intrigued by it, it was not until the middle of the nineteenth century that serious interest in Buddhism developed and detailed knowledge of its teachings became available.

Knowledge of Buddhism has come through three main channels: the labour of Western scholars; the work of philosophers, intellectuals, writers, and artists; and the arrival of Asian immigrants who have brought various forms of Buddhism with them to America and Europe.

Academic Study

Academic interest in Buddhism developed during the colonial period, as European officials—many of them proficient amateur scholars—were posted to different parts of Asia. The earliest Buddhist texts to be studied were Mahāyāna Sanskrit manuscripts collected in Nepal by the British Resident, B. H. Hodgson. Another British civil servant who made an outstanding contribution to the study of Theravāda Buddhism was T. W. Rhys Davids (1843–1922). Rhys Davids became interested in Buddhism during his residence in Sri Lanka and went on to found the Pali Text Society in 1881. The Society remains to this day the most important outlet for the publication of texts and translations of Pali Buddhist literature.

Professional scholars from many countries played an important role in the transmission of Buddhism to the West. In 1845 the Frenchman Eugène Burnouf published his *Introduction to the History of Indian Buddhism* and followed this seven years later with a translation of the *Lotus Sūtra*. Interest in Buddhism in Germany was stimulated by the publication of Herman Oldenberg's *The Buddha, His Life, His Doctrine, His Community* in 1881. Close to the end of the century the American Henry Clarke Warren published his *Buddhism in Translations* (1896) a fine anthology of material from the Pali Canon which has remained popular to the present day. Around this time the first Parliament of the World's Religions was held in Chicago in 1893, an event designed to bring representatives of the different world faiths together to explore the common ground they shared. The Buddhist representatives included Anagarika Dharmapala (1864–1933), a Sri Lankan who made a great impression in his speeches and public meetings. He made two further visits within the next ten years and founded an American branch of the recently established Maha Bodhi Society, the first international Buddhist association which had its headquarters in Calcutta. The American offshoot of the Society was the first Buddhist organization in the West. Shortly after the turn of the century attention broadened from south Asian Buddhism to include the study of Mahāyāna Buddhism through Tibetan and Chinese sources. The great Belgian scholars Louis de La Vallée Poussin and (later) Étienne Lamotte made an enormous contribution in this field. Mention must also be made of D. T. Suzuki (1870–1966), a Japanese Buddhist who promoted awareness of Zen Buddhism through his lectures and influential books.

Philosophy, Culture, and the Arts

The second way Buddhism has entered Western culture is through philosophy, culture, and the arts. The German philosopher Arthur Schopenhauer (1788–1860) was the first major Western thinker to take an interest in Buddhism. Due to the absence of reliable sources, Schopenhauer had only an imperfect knowledge of Buddhism, and saw it as confirming his own somewhat pessimistic philosophy. Of all the world religions Buddhism seemed to him the most rational and ethically evolved, and the frequent references to Buddhism in his writings brought it to the attention of Western intellectuals in the latter part of the nineteenth century.

In England, Sir Edwin Arnold (1832–1904) published his famous poem *The Light of Asia* in 1879. The poem describes the life and teachings of the Buddha in a melodramatic style which made it very popular with middle-class Victorian audiences on both sides of the Atlantic. Arnold was a Christian who saw much in common in the teachings of Jesus and the Buddha. He visited the site of the Buddha's enlightenment at Bodh Gayā in 1885 and campaigned for funds to restore it from its dilapidated condition. Around this time interest in the supernatural among the Victorians was at its height, and in 1875 Colonel Henry Olcott (1832–1907) and Madame Blavatsky (1831–91) founded the Theosophical Society which was devoted to uncovering the esoteric truth believed to lie at the heart of all religions.

Attention was focused mainly on the religions of the East, and Buddhism in particular became a popular subject of study and discussion in salons and drawing-rooms.

The German novelist Herman Hesse often alluded to Buddhist themes in his writings, notably in his 1922 novel *Siddhartha*, which has been translated into many languages. In the post-war years Jack Kerouac's novels *The Dharma Bums* and *On the Road* were popular with the 'Beat' generation and provided inspiration for the counter-cultures of subsequent decades. The eclectic thinker and philosopher Alan Watts wrote a number of books on Zen which attracted a popular readership, but perhaps more than any other single work Robert M. Persig's *Zen and the Art of Motorcycle Maintenance* (1974)—although more concerned with Western philosophy than Zen—has ensured that this school of Buddhism is widely known in the West, at least by name. The cinema, too, has played its part in infusing Buddhist ideas into Western culture. Hesse's novel *Siddhartha* was made into a film which became very popular on college campuses in the 1970s. More recently, the plot of Bertolucci's *Little Buddha*, shot partly in India and partly in America, illustrates the extent to which Buddhism is becoming part of Western culture. The plot interweaves the life story of the Buddha with the quest for a Tibetan lama who has been reborn in Seattle to American parents.

Buddhist Immigration

The third channel for the introduction of Buddhism to the West has been immigration. This is a phenomenon which has affected the United States and Europe in different ways. The majority of Buddhist immigration has been to the United States, and began as early as the 1860s when Chinese labourers arrived to work on the railroads and in the gold mines. Immigrants from both China and Japan settled in

Hawaii before it was formally annexed by the United States in 1898. Recent decades have seen an influx of immigrants from Indo-China in the wake of the Vietnam war, and perhaps half a million Buddhists from South-East Asia have settled in the USA. The tendency has been for immigrant communities to establish their own local temples as a means of preserving their distinctive cultural identity rather than for proselytizing purposes. Only after the first or second generation does a pattern of interaction with the host community develop such that individuals from different cultural backgrounds meet as 'Buddhists' rather than as members of a particular ethnic group.

Although the United Kingdom has received large numbers of Asian immigrants these have come mainly from the Indian subcontinent and are mostly Hindus or Muslims. There are some 19,000 refugees from Indo-China in Britain, 22,000 in Germany, and 97,000 in France. The majority of Buddhists in Europe are Caucasians who have converted to Buddhism rather than immigrants who brought their beliefs with them. Although accurate numbers are difficult to come by, in the UK there are around a hundred Tibetan centres, about ninety Theravāda centres, and some forty Zen centres, together with a further hundred or so other groups including the Friends of the Western Buddhist Order. Converts to Buddhism in both Europe and the United States come predominantly from the middle classes.

All the major forms of Buddhism are now represented in the West, but statistics on the rate of growth of Buddhism are difficult to come by, and there are wide variations in the figures quoted. In his pioneering study *American Buddhism*, Charles Prebish estimated the number of Buddhists in the United States in 1979 as something in the order of a few hundred thousand. Less than ten years later in 1987 the American Buddhist Congress, a body founded in the same year with forty-five affiliated groups, put the figure at 3–5 million. No census of Buddhist groups and organizations in the United States has been undertaken, but Prebish estimates there are now about a thousand such groups. The increase in the popularity of Buddhism can also be seen elsewhere in the West, although the growth has generally been less spectacular in Europe than in the USA. Estimates suggest there are over a million Buddhists in Europe, with about 200,000 in the UK and an equivalent number in France.

Buddhist Schools in the West

To date, Buddhism has presented many different faces to the West. The first form of Buddhism to appeal to a mass audience was Zen, which became popular in America after the Second World War. Many Americans encountered Japanese culture while stationed in the country during military service. Zen has had a strong appeal in America: its emphasis on spontaneity, simplicity, and direct personal experience resonated with cultural trends in post-war America. The iconoclastic and anti-authoritarian spirit of Zen appealed also to the 1950s 'Beat' generation, and the 'Hippy' movement of the 1960s. Those who experimented with LSD and other psychedelic drugs such as mescalin often did so in the context of a spiritually motivated quest for the 'mind-expanding' experience they conceived enlightenment to be.

Japanese schools other than Zen are also well represented in the West. One of the earliest and most popular was the Jōdo Shinshū (True Pure Land School) which was established in Honolulu in 1899. Many of the early Japanese immigrants to the United States were followers of this school, and for many decades its members comprised the majority of Japanese–American Buddhists. More recently, one of the fastest-growing groups in America and Europe has been Soka Gakkai International. Soka Gakkai ('value-creation society') was originally the lay wing of Nichiren-

Shōshū, but separated from it early in the 1990s. Soka Gakkai International actively seeks converts and has achieved a growth rate similar to that of evangelical Christianity, which it resembles somewhat in its positive and upbeat gospel of 'good news'. Its teaching that individuals can achieve all their goals through frequent repetition of the mantra *Namu myōhō renge kyō* ('Honour to the *Lotus Sūtra* of the True Dharma') coupled with a positive mental attitude, has proved popular with those attracted to a more optimistic, 'world-affirming' strain of Buddhism. The rock artist Tina Turner is a member of this sect.

Tibetan Buddhism provides a striking contrast with the elegant simplicity of Zen. The rituals, symbols, and ceremonials of Tibetan Buddhism generate a powerful sense of what Rudolf Otto called the 'numinous', or the apprehension of the supernatural as mysterious and uncanny. Tibetan rituals invoke the numinous through the use of chanting, *maṇḍalas*, *mantras*, mystic symbols, ritual implements, candles, incense, and dramatic sounds such as the clashing of cymbals. Teachings are revealed gradually in the course of a series of hierarchical initiations. In the Western imagination, Tibet has long been the epicentre of Eastern mysticism, and the opportunity to meet native teachers from 'the land of snows' and participate in the rituals of an ancient culture is attractive to those who find Western civilization increasingly bereft of spiritual content.

The invasion of Tibet in 1950 triggered a Tibetan diaspora which included many high lamas who were subsequently resettled by Buddhist groups in the West, where all the major Tibetan schools are now represented. Charismatic Tibetan teachers such as Chogyam Trungpa (1939–87) began a dialogue with Western psychology regarding the spiritual dimension of the human psyche. The potential for collaboration between Buddhism and humanistic psychology is great, and this may be one of the major channels through which Buddhism enters mainstream Western culture. Trungpa founded centres such as the one at Boulder, Colorado, and later assumed responsibility for its sister institute at Samye Ling in Scotland, founded by Ānanda Bodhi.

The Western media has also kept Tibet in the headlines through its coverage of political and human rights issues, and many Westerners have participated in rallies and protests against the Chinese occupation. The support of celebrities and film stars such as Richard Gere and Harrison Ford, the frequent appearances of His Holiness the Dalai Lama, and investigations by government agencies and international panels of jurists have all served to raise the profile of Tibet in the West.

Chinese forms of Buddhism are particularly well represented in the United States due in large part to the arrival of immigrants, as noted above. In 1962 Tripitaka Master Hsuan Hua arrived from Hong Kong and shortly afterwards established the Sino-American Buddhist Association in San Francisco in 1968. Before long a majority of the membership was comprised of American Caucasians, and the organization moved to larger headquarters at 'The City of 10,000 Buddhas' in northern California where a school and university were set up along with monastic training institutes. The honour of being the largest Buddhist temple in the Western hemisphere is claimed by the Taiwan-based Hsi Lai temple in Los Angeles.

The first Theravāda institution in the United States was established in Washington DC in 1966, and there are now twenty or more monasteries populated by monks from Sri Lanka, Burma, Laos, Thailand, Cambodia, and America. Theravāda Buddhism has been present in England for almost a hundred years, although its low-key style and preference for simple manners over charismatic leadership has meant that its profile has remained low. Theravāda was the first form of Buddhism to appear in the West, and in keeping with the cyclic nature of things is currently undergoing something of a renaissance. Interest in Pali, the language of the Theravāda texts, has increased in recent years, and the availability of electronic editions of the Pali Canon has provided a stimulus to research. New and vigorous Theravāda centres have also sprung up, such as the Amarāvatī Buddhist Centre near Hemel Hempstead in England. This was founded in 1985 under the leadership of the American monk Ajahn Sumedho, a pupil of the Thai monk Ajahn Chaa.

The Popularity of Buddhism

Why has Buddhism proved so popular in the West? The reasons for this are complex, and have as much to do with the cultural history of the West as with the attractions of Buddhism. Various Western 'readings' of Buddhism have been popular from time to time, and that often these tell us more about changing fashions in the West than they do about Buddhism. One of the most popular Western interpretations of Buddhism is as a rational philosophy, and developments in the West have created a climate which is favourable to Buddhism when seen in this light. The dominant cultural influences in the West since the Enlightenment in the eighteenth century have been science and secular liberalism. Buddhism *qua* rational philosophy seems compatible with both of these, at least to a greater extent than has been the case with orthodox Western religion. Scientific discoveries, and theories such as evolution, have challenged many traditional Christian teachings, and the long rearguard action fought by established religion in defence of revealed 'truths' has made it seem dogmatic, irrational, and backward-looking. The absence of an anthropomorphic concept of deity is another feature which makes Buddhism more acceptable to the modern mind.

By contrast there seem few Buddhist doctrines which are

in direct conflict with science, and proponents of Buddhist rationalism have offered allegorical interpretations of any which are. The Buddhist world-view is less parochial than the universe of traditional Christianity and, if anything, seems to anticipate the findings of modern cosmology rather than be in conflict with them. Recent discoveries in quantum physics, furthermore, suggest that science is slowly coming to a view of reality not unlike that described in Buddhist philosophy. Books such as Frijof Capra's *The Tao of Physics* (1976) have revealed interesting parallels between the conceptual worlds of theoretical physics and Eastern thought.

Even belief in reincarnation—perhaps the most difficult Buddhist concept for Westerners to accept—has received empirical support in studies such as those by the American psychiatrist Ian Stevenson, notably in his book *Twenty Cases Suggestive of Reincarnation* (1974). Belief in reincarnation is widespread in many cultures, and in the post-Christian West the idea is once again becoming part of popular culture. Many people have experimented with past life regression under hypnosis and claim to recall experiences from previous existences. Whatever the truth of the matter, the notion of reincarnation is intriguing and adds an interesting new perspective on human life which many find appealing.

One of the implications of reincarnation is that individuals can transmigrate through different species, for example as when a human being is reborn as an animal, or vice versa. This provides a new perspective on the relationship between man and the rest of creation, one very much in tune with contemporary ecology. In the traditional Christian view man is the caretaker or custodian of the natural world, answerable to God for the discharge of his duty, but otherwise free to exercise dominion over the natural order. Many ecologists see this belief as having encouraged the over-exploitation of nature and having fostered an attitude of indifference to the well-being of other species. The Christian teaching that only man has an immortal soul, and there is no place in heaven for animals, seems 'speciesist' and out of keeping with the holistic tenor of much contemporary thought. Unlike Christianity, Buddhism draws no hard and fast line between different forms of life. Although it recognizes that human life has a special value, it acknowledges that all living creatures are entitled to respect in their own right, not simply because of the utility they may possess for human beings.

Buddhism also seems in harmony with the other dominant contemporary Western ideology, namely secular liberalism. Buddhism is undogmatic, even to the extent of instructing its followers not to accept its own teachings uncritically but always to test them in the light of their own experience. Although it asks that its followers take certain basic teachings on trust in the initial stages, and adopt a positive and open-minded attitude, Buddhism is more concerned with the development of understanding than the acceptance of credal formulas. The fact that Buddhism imposes few confessional, ritual, or other requirements on its followers makes it easy to live as a Buddhist in a pluralistic milieu and minimizes the likelihood of overt conflict with secular values. Perhaps this aspect of Buddhism has contributed to its popularity in the USA, where Church and State are constitutionally separate.

Buddhism is also perceived as liberal and progressive in the field of ethics. Its moral teachings are not expressed as commandments in the imperative form 'Thou shalt not' but as rational principles which if followed will lead to the good and happiness of oneself and others. The Buddhist toleration of alternative viewpoints contrasts with the some of the darker episodes in the history of Western religion, where persecution and torture have been employed in order to stamp out heresy. Westerners who object to the dogmatic moralizing tone of established religion often find Buddhism a congenial alternative within which to pursue their religious goals. Meditation also has a strong appeal, and offers practical techniques for dealing with stress and other psychosomatic problems.

Buddhist Modernism

The fact that Buddhism can be presented as in harmony with influential contemporary ideologies has undoubtedly aided its spread in the West. This reading of Buddhism, however, which has been termed 'Buddhist modernism', suppresses certain features of the religion which have been present since the earliest times which are less in harmony with contemporary Western attitudes. The belief in miracles and in the efficacy of *mantras*, spells, and charms is one such example. Even today, the Tibetan government in exile consults the state oracle for advice on important matters. Belief in the existence of otherworldly realms populated by gods and spirits, and in the unseen power of karma, are other tenets which have been central to Buddhist teachings from the earliest times.

The traditional Buddhist view of the status of women is also problematic. Many feminists see all religion as inherently patriarchal and repressive, but where Buddhism is concerned the picture is more complex. Buddhism is a product of a traditional Asian society, one in which women were regarded as subservient to men. Largely due to these cultural associations Buddhism may fairly be described as 'androcentric', and there is certainly a tendency in many sources to see rebirth as a female as a relative misfortune. Perhaps this is due not so much to overt discrimination as a reflection of the fact that the lot of women in certain Asian cultures has been—and remains—unenviable. However, it would be wrong to generalize about Asian culture in this respect. As compared to pre-modern Europe, the position of women was far better in legal and other terms in such countries as

Burma than in the West. Furthermore, Buddhism does not believe there is any obstacle other than of a social nature to women making spiritual progress. Indeed, Buddhism was one of the first religions to institute a religious order of nuns, although the Buddha was at first reluctant to allow this, feeling, perhaps, that society was not yet ready for such an innovative development.

From a philosophical perspective, many influential Buddhist texts make the point that gender, like all other natural attributes, lacks inherent reality. This undercuts the basis for discrimination against women as far as Buddhist philosophy is concerned. In spite of its acceptance of gender-equality at a philosophical level, however, Buddhism may need to modify certain of its traditional rituals and customs to accommodate the free mingling of the sexes which is customary in the West. An organization known as Sakyadhita ('daughters of the Buddha'), an international association of Buddhist women, exists to unite Buddhist women of various countries and traditions.

A Buddhist Enlightenment?

Other areas of potential conflict between Buddhism and Western thought still remain, and many differences have been papered over rather than squarely faced by modernist interpreters. What seems called for is a 'Buddhist Enlightenment', that is to say a systematic updating of the intellectual foundations of the religion so as to allow a clear and consistent set of teachings on modern issues to emerge. In the last decade or so a broadly based movement known as 'socially engaged Buddhism' has begun the attempt to address questions of a social, political, and moral nature. Based around the teachings of the Vietnamese monk Thich Nhat Hanh, the movement seeks ways to apply the ancient teachings to the challenges of modern life. This is no easy task, since to a large extent Buddhism is a pre-modern phenomenon and has little experience of the problems that life in the West presents. One of the most important centres of Buddhist culture—Tibet—was a medieval theocracy until half a century ago, almost entirely cut off from the outside world. Buddhism in the rest of Asia has been largely geared to the needs of agricultural peasant communities where the village and the monastery live in symbiosis. The problems which arise in these contexts are not the same as those faced by residents of urban communities in the West, where there is no consensus on religious and moral issues and where the individual functions as an atomic unit rather than within a network of kinship relations. The success with which Buddhism is able to reinvent itself for the West will determine the extent to which it becomes a mainstream religious force.

A New Buddhism for the West?

'Why should there not be in time a Western Buddhism, a Nava-yana or "new vehicle" . . . not deliberately formed as such but a natural growth from the same roots of Buddhism as all others, that is, the record of the Buddha's Enlightenment? There is no reason why it should not grow happily alongside, and even blend with the best of Western science, psychology and social science, and thus affect the ever-changing field of Western thought. It will not be Theravāda or Zen . . . Just what it will be we do not know, nor does it matter at the present time. The Dhamma as such is immortal, but its forms must ever change to serve the ever-changing human need.'

The above are the words of Christmas Humphreys (1901–83), the founder-president of the Buddhist Society in England. They are taken from his book *Sixty Years of Buddhism in England*, p. 80.

The dilemma Buddhism faces is not unique, and contemporary developments in other religions provide an interesting parallel. It would not be unprecedented if the tensions within Buddhism led to a split between conservative and progressive factions similar to the division between the orthodox and liberal wings of Judaism. Perhaps history will repeat itself, and the arrival of Buddhism in the West will provoke a modern version of the 'Great Schism' which occurred in the third century BC between liberals and conservatives. One group dedicated to the development of a distinctive Western form of Buddhism is the UK-based Friends of the Western Buddhist Order (FWBO). Members of the group live in communities and are dedicated to the evolution of an alternative society supported by co-operatives run in accordance with Buddhist principles.

Recent developments in information technology are another factor which will influence the spread of Buddhism. The emergence of the 'CyberSangha'—a network of Buddhist groups in the United States linked by computers—and the availability of online information about Buddhism through electronic media such as the *Journal of Buddhist Ethics*, means that individuals across the globe now have access via the Internet to a 'virtual' Buddhist community of a kind which has never existed before. The existence of a global information network should go a long way to reducing misunderstandings of the kind experienced by the blind men in their encounter with the elephant.

The historian Arnold Toynbee described the encounter between Buddhism and the West as 'one of the greatest collisions of the twenty-first century'. To this confluence of cultures Buddhism brings a sophisticated psychology, techniques of meditation, a profound metaphysics, and a universally admired code of ethics. The West brings a sceptical empiricism, a pragmatic science and technology, and a commitment to democracy and individual liberty. If the history of the spread of Buddhism to other cultures teaches any lessons it is that a genuinely new and distinctive form of Buddhism will be born from this encounter.

Timeline

500–600	Development of Tantric Buddhism (Vajrayāna)
	Buddhism arrives in Japan
618–917	T'ang dynasty (China)
600–700	Buddhism arrives in Tibet
794–1185	Heian period (Japan)
900–1000	Invasion of north India by Turkish Muslim tribes
c.1000	Buddhism arrives in Thailand (may have come earlier)
1044–77	Reign of Anawrahta (Burma)
1185–1333	Kamakura period (Japan)
1173–1262	Shinran
c.1200	Nālandā university sacked for the last time
c.1100–1200	Zen arrives in Japan from China and Korea
1222–82	Nichiren
1200–1300	Buddhism disappears from India
	Marco Polo travels to China
1287	Sack of Pagan by Mongols (Burma)
1357–1410	Life of Tsong-kha-pa
c.1850	Beginning of Western interest in Buddhism
1881	Pali Text Society founded
1907	Buddhist Society of Great Britain and Ireland founded
1950	Invasion of Tibet by Chinese
1959	Dalai Lama flees Tibet after failed uprising
1966	Cultural Revolution (China)
1987	American Buddhist Congress founded

Further Reading

There are many good introductory books on Buddhism which can be used to supplement the basic sketch provided in this volume. One of the most recent and comprehensive, with the benefit of an excellent bibliography, is:

Peter Harvey, *An Introduction to Buddhism. Teachings, History and Practices* (Cambridge, 1990).

Other useful volumes are:

Edward Conze, *A Short Introduction to Buddhism* (London, 1980).

R. H. Robinson and W. L. Johnson, *The Buddhist Religion: A Historical Introduction* (Belmont, Calif., 1982).

A lavishly illustrated introduction with chapters contributed by a range of specialists on the various Buddhist cultures is:

Heinz Bechert and Richard Gombrich (eds.), *The World of Buddhism: Buddhist Monks and Nuns in Society and Culture* (London, 1984).

A very good short introduction to the Buddha's life and social context may be found in:

M. Carrithers, *The Buddha* (Oxford, 1983).

For an illuminating guide to the spread of Buddhism:

E. Zürcher, *Buddhism, its Origins and Spread in Words, Maps and Pictures* (New York, 1962).

For an excellent introduction to Theravāda Buddhism see:

Richard Gombrich, *Theravada Buddhism: A Social History from Ancient Benares to Modern Colombo* (London, 1988).

A simple, lucid explanation of the basic doctrines of Theravāda Buddhism can be found in:

Walpola Rahula, *What the Buddha Taught* (Bedford, 1959).

For a more advanced account of Mahāyāna Buddhism than can be found in any of the sources already mentioned see:

Paul Williams, *Mahayana Buddhism: The Doctrinal Foundations* (London, 1989).

The subject of Buddhist art and iconography is covered in:
D. L. Snellgrove (ed.), *The Image of the Buddha* (London, 1978).

Tantric Buddhism is discussed in:
S. Dasgupta, *An Introduction to Tantric Buddhism* (Berkeley, 1974).
J. Blofeld, *The Tantric Mysticism of Tibet: A Practical Guide* (Boston, 1987).

On Buddhism in China:
Ch'en, K. K. S, *Buddhism in China: A Historical Survey* (Princeton, 1964).
E. Zürcher, *The Buddhist Conquest of China* (Leiden, 1959).

Buddhism in Japan is treated in:
J. M. Kitagawa, *Religion in Japanese History* (New York, 1966).

On Buddhist meditation:
Winston King, *Theravada Meditation: The Buddhist Transformation of Yoga* (University Park, Pennsylvania, 1980).
L. Kornfield, *Living Buddhist Masters* (Boulder, Colorado, 1983).
H. Saddhatissa, *The Buddha's Way* (London, 1971).

A good, practical guide to Buddhist meditation is:
Kathleen McDonald, *How to Meditate* (London, 1984).

On ethics:
H. Saddhatissa, *Buddhist Ethics: Essence of Buddhism* (London, 1987).
Roshi Philip Aitken, *The Mind of Clover: Essays in Zen Buddhist Ethics* (Berkeley, 1984).
Information about the online *Journal of Buddhist Ethics*, edited by the author and Charles S. Prebish, can be obtained by sending an email message to *jbe-ed@psu.edu* or visiting the journal's World Wide Web sites at http: / / www.psu.edu/jbe/jbe.html (USA) or
http: / / www.gold.ac.uk/jbe/jbe.html (UK).

For further discussion of the kind of issues in medical ethics raised in Chapter 4:
Damien Keown, *Buddhism & Bioethics* (London, 1995).

William LaFleur, *Liquid Life: Abortion and Buddhism in Japan* (Princeton, 1992).

On the role of women in Buddhism:

Rita M. Gross, *Buddhism After Patriarchy: A Feminist History, Analysis, and Reconstruction of Buddhism* (Albany, NY, 1993).

The following discuss various aspects of the role of Buddhism in the modern world:

P. C. Almond, *The British Discovery of Buddhism* (Cambridge, 1988).

H. Dumoulin (ed.), *Buddhism in the Modern World* (London, 1962).

C. Humphreys, *Sixty Years of Buddhism in England (1907-1967)*, (London, 1968).

T. Kashima, *Buddhism in America: the Social Organization of an Ethnic Religious Institution* (London, 1977).

Ken Jones, *The Social Face of Buddhism* (London, 1989).

Charles S. Prebish, *American Buddhism* (Belmont, Calif., 1979).

Charles S. Prebish, *Buddhism: A Modern Perspective* (University Park, Pennsylvania, 1975).

Dharmachari Subhuti, *Buddhism for Today: A Portrait of a New Buddhist Movement* (Salisbury, 1983).

Chogyam Trungpa, *Cutting Through Spiritual Materialism* (Berkeley, 1983).

Links to online sources of information about Buddhism can be found at the Global Resources Center at the *Journal of Buddhist Ethics* World Wide Web sites, at the address above.

The best way to learn about Buddhism is to read the Buddha's teachings. The standard complete translation of the Pali Canon, by various authors, is that published by the Pali Text Society. Two translations of parts of the Buddha's early discourses are:

Maurice Walshe, *The Long Discourses of the Buddha* (Boston, 1995).

Bhikkhu Ñāṇamoli and Bhikkhu Bodhi, *The Middle Length Discourses of the Buddha* (Boston, 1995).

Index

MORE OXFORD PAPERBACKS

This book is just one of nearly 1000 Oxford Paperbacks currently in print. If you would like details of other Oxford Paperbacks, including titles in the World's Classics, Oxford Reference, Oxford Books, OPUS, Past Masters, Oxford Authors, and Oxford Shakespeare series, please write to:

UK and Europe: Oxford Paperbacks Publicity Manager, Arts and Reference Publicity Department, Oxford University Press, Walton Street, Oxford OX2 6DP.

Customers in UK and Europe will find Oxford Paperbacks available in all good bookshops. But in case of difficulty please send orders to the Cash-with-Order Department, Oxford University Press Distribution Services, Saxon Way West, Corby, Northants NN18 9ES. Tel: 01536 741519; Fax: 01536 746337. Please send a cheque for the total cost of the books, plus £1.75 postage and packing for orders under £20; £2.75 for orders over £20. Customers outside the UK should add 10% of the cost of the books for postage and packing.

USA: Oxford Paperbacks Marketing Manager, Oxford University Press, Inc., 200 Madison Avenue, New York, N.Y. 10016.

Canada: Trade Department, Oxford University Press, 70 Wynford Drive, Don Mills, Ontario M3C 1J9.

Australia: Trade Marketing Manager, Oxford University Press, G.P.O. Box 2784Y, Melbourne 3001, Victoria.

South Africa: Oxford University Press, P.O. Box 1141, Cape Town 8000.

A Very Short Introduction

CLASSICS

Mary Beard and John Henderson

This *Very Short Introduction* to Classics links a haunting temple on a lonely mountainside to the glory of ancient Greece and the grandeur of Rome, and to Classics within modern culture—from Jefferson and Byron to Asterix and Ben-Hur.

'This little book should be in the hands of every student, and every tourist to the lands of the ancient world . . . a splendid piece of work'
Peter Wiseman
Author of *Talking to Virgil*

'an eminently readable and useful guide to many of the modern debates enlivening the field . . . the most up-to-date and accessible introduction available'
Edith Hall
Author of *Inventing the Barbarian*

'lively and up-to-date . . . it shows classics as a living enterprise, not a warehouse of relics'
New Statesman and Society

'nobody could fail to be informed and entertained—the accent of the book is provocative and stimulating'
Times Literary Supplement

POLITICS

Kenneth Minogue

Since politics is both complex and controversial it is easy to miss the wood for the trees. In this Very Short Introduction Kenneth Minogue has brought the many dimensions of politics into a single focus: he discusses both the everyday grind of democracy and the attraction of grand ideals such as freedom and justice.

'Kenneth Minogue is a very lively stylist who does not distort difficult ideas.'
Maurice Cranston

'a dazzling but unpretentious display of great scholarship and humane reflection'
Professor Neil O'Sullivan, University of Hull

'Minogue is an admirable choice for showing us the nuts and bolts of the subject.'
Nicholas Lezard, *Guardian*

'This is a fascinating book which sketches, in a very short space, one view of the nature of politics . . . the reader is challenged, provoked and stimulated by Minogue's trenchant views.'
Talking Politics

JUDAISM

Norman Solomon

'Norman Solomon has achieved the near impossible with his enlightened very short introduction to Judaism. Since it is well known that Judaism is almost impossible to summarize, and that there are as many different opinions about Jewish matters as there are Jews, this is a small masterpiece in its success in representing various shades of Jewish opinion, often mutually contradictory. Solomon also manages to keep the reader engaged, never patronizes, assumes little knowledge but a keen mind, and takes us through Jewish life and history with such gusto that one feels enlivened, rather than exhausted, at the end.'
Rabbi Julia Neuberger

'This book will serve a very useful purpose indeed. I'll use it myself to discuss, to teach, agree with, and disagree with, in the Jewish manner!'
Rabbi Lionel Blue

'A magnificent achievement. Dr Solomon's treatment, fresh, very readable, witty and stimulating, will delight everyone interested in religion in the modern world.'
Dr Louis Jacobs, University of London